HOME AND NATIVE LAND

HOME AND NATIVE LAND

Aboriginal Rights and the Canadian Constitution

MICHAEL ASCH

∩ METHUEN

Toronto New York London Sydney Auckland

Canadian Cataloguing in Publication Data

Asch, Michael.
    Home and native land

ISBN 0-458-97380-7

1. Indians of North America - Canada - Civil rights.
2. Indians of North America - Canada - Government
relations.   3. Indians of North America - Canada -
Land tenure.   4. Indians of North America - Canada -
Legal status, laws, etc.   I. Title.

E92.A82   1984   323.1′197′071   C83-099311-8

Printed and bound in Canada

  2 3 4   84   88 87 86 85

CONTENTS

Prologue　vii

1/Introduction: A Problem Defined　1
　Aboriginal Peoples　2
　Existing Aboriginal Rights　5
　Conclusions and Summary of Chapters　8

2/Contemporary Native Life: Images and Realities　13
　Introduction　13
　The Dene　14
　Some Comparisons　20
　Conclusions　22

3/Aboriginal Rights: The View of the Aboriginal Peoples　26
　The Definition of Aboriginal Rights　27
　Summary and Conclusion　37

4/The Discovery of Aboriginal Rights in the Law　41
　English Colonial Law and Ethnocentrism　42
　The Acquisition of a New Territory　43
　The Canadian Situation　46
　Conclusions: Aboriginal Rights and the Law　53

5/The Evolution of Federal Policy on Aboriginal Rights　55
　Land Acquisition Policy Prior to the Calder Case　56
　　State Acknowledgement of a Native Interest　57
　　The Government's View of the Content of the Native
　　　Interest　59
　Claims Policy After the Calder Case　64
　　The Native Interest: Post-Calder　66
　Summary　68
　Conclusions: Current Policy and its Evolution　71

6/Aboriginal Rights in the Context of Canadian Democracy　74
　Some Characteristics of Liberal-Democracy　75
　Ethnonational Political Rights in Belgium and Switzerland　77
　Ethnonational Political Rights in Canada　82
　Conclusions　87

7/From Theory to Practice   89
    The Southern Approach   90
    The Approach of the Northwest Territories   93
    Nunavut: The Perspective of the Nunavut Constitutional
        Forum   95
    Denendeh: The Perspective of the Dene Nation and the Metis
        Association   96
    Reconciling the Proposals with Canadian
        Political Ideology   100
    Conclusions   104

Appendix
    A Constitution Act, 1982   111
    B The Royal Proclamation, 1763   112
    C Treaty No. 4   115
    D A Comparison of Provincial Powers and the Powers of
       Indian Bands under the Indian Act   121
    E Declaration of The First Nations   125
    F Metis Declaration of Rights   126
    G Dene Declaration   127
    H Declaration on the Granting of Independence to Colonial
       Countries and Peoples   129
    I International Covenant on the Rights of Indigenous
       Peoples   132
    J Proposed 1984 Constitutional Accord on the Rights of
       the Aboriginal Peoples of Canada   139
    K A Guide to Further Readings   140

Suggested Readings   143

Bibliography   146

Cases and Statutes   153

Index   154

PROLOGUE

This book discusses self-determination and self-government of the aboriginal peoples of Canada. It addresses issues that concern specific proposals advanced by various native organizations and how these might be accommodated within existing constitutional arrangements. It does not discuss, except in passing, matters that relate to hunting, fishing and trapping rights, or whether native peoples need comply with such laws as provincial game regulations; nor does it focus on treaty rights. These are matters that, it is hoped, will soon be addressed elsewhere.

The choice to focus on questions of political rights was easy to make. As will become evident as the book progresses, this issue is most central both to the aboriginal organizations and to the government. But my reasons for this choice go further: they flow from my own view that unless matters concerning political rights and self-government are resolved, or at least understood to be resolvable within a mutually agreed framework, the settlement of issues such as land rights, hunting, fishing and trapping rights, and treaty rights (or rights obtained through express agreement with the Crown) can only proceed on an *ad hoc* basis. In short, in my mind, an understanding about the nature of these rights must come first (even if, as is often the case in negotiations, the specifics are concluded only after other matters have been dealt with).

The primary audience to whom I direct my words are those individuals who are interested in the subject but who feel a lack of background information necessary to form firm opinions, especially on such thorny issues as political rights. One objective, then, is to supply such information from disciplines as diverse as law, history, native studies, anthropology, economics and political science. I have tried to present an accurate portrait of what the information contains; however, I must make it plain that I have not done so from a neutral stance. I am convinced that the entrenchment of political rights for aboriginal governments is essential, and that this goal can be accommodated within Confederation; the information is organized with this in mind. Still, my intention is to present what I consider to be an objective and accurate account and, as much as possible, let the conclusions arise from the facts presented. Whether I have been successful is a question others must answer.

It would not be wrong to state that I came to the knowledge I have on this subject because I decided to write the book. But this is not the whole story. I am an anthropologist, and my experiences from the time of my first fieldwork among the Dene (Athapaskan-speaking peoples of the Mackenzie River Valley) in 1969 at Fort Wrigley, Northwest Territories, to the initiation of serious research on this volume in 1982 have all contributed to the process of acquiring knowledge.

Of these experiences, two stand out. The most significant is the research I have undertaken for the Dene Nation (the political organization that represents the Dene of the Mackenzie River Valley), which includes the preparation of testimony on matters such as economic history, land use and socioeconomic impact assessment for numerous boards, hearings and inquiries (such as the Mackenzie Valley Pipeline Inquiry under Mr. Justice Thomas R. Berger). In the past five years, I have been involved in the preparation of position papers on land claims, economic and political institutions, and government policy for use in their aboriginal-rights claims negotiations. This research has given me the opportunity to delve into questions of government policy and the law and the positions of various aboriginal organizations on the subject of their rights. Much of what I write in the descriptive chapters, then, originates in research that was undertaken earlier for the Dene Nation.

The second important source of experience is my academic life. In the fall of 1980 I decided to develop a course on the subject of aboriginal rights and the Dene. It was intended, in large part, to guide me to a more systematic understanding of the issues involved than I had gained through my work with the Dene Nation. To prepare for this course, I went through much of the literature available on legal, political, historical and other questions related to the subject. In January 1981, I presented it for the first time, with the voluntary help of a number of individuals from the university and native communities. By the time I taught the course for a second time, I felt confident that I could render the material into written form.

One factor that convinced me that it was the appropriate time to write on aboriginal rights was the position of the federal government in 1982. Their view, which I gleaned from newspaper accounts, press releases and contact through the claims process, was simply to deny vociferously that aboriginal peoples had "special" political rights. It was clear from the strength of the rhetoric that the recognition of these rights would not be entertained in the near future. As a person who is strongly committed to the idea that such rights ought to be accommodated within Confederation, I was motivated to present my own analysis on the subject, and was delighted when Methuen gave me the opportunity to do so.

The past eighteen months, however, have brought about a remarkable change in the attitude of government. At the time of writing (December 1983), its position has moved from what could best be termed entrenched resistance to one of reluctant and sceptical acceptance. Thus a book that I assumed would present a radical critique of government has become much more moderate in stance. But it is not the argument that has changed, only the position of government. It is a change that, in my view, can be attributed to the effective work done by the organizations that represent the aboriginal nations. Although beyond the scope of this book, it is a story that merits detailed treatment.

The second important change is the change in my own attitude. At the outset, I was convinced that certain proposals put forward by aboriginal organizations were inimicable to the tenets of liberal-democracy. I believed I would find myself uncomfortable in presenting them. My initial solution was to avoid this issue by focussing attention on the one proposal I felt best overcame these objections: that of the Dene Nation. As it happens, I discovered, in the process of writing this volume, that my initial objections were incorrect and so the final version of the book pays much more attention to other proposals than I intended at the start of writing.

The final modification is the inclusion of the argument that convinced me to change my opinion. When I first contemplated how I would present my case in the text, I rejected the idea of comparing the situation of native peoples of Canada with other similar situations in the world. My reasoning was based on observation. Usually the comparison advanced is between Canadian native peoples and those of the United States, New Zealand and Denmark (Greenland). It is one which I raised in my classes, but found that it resulted not in a clarification of the issues nor an advancement of the argument, but rather in the creation of additional questions that needed answers. I therefore decided not to lose any time on the subject of comparisons but jump from a discourse on the general argument (as now outlined in Chapter 5) to specific proposals (as now contained in Chapter 7), in particular those of the Dene.

Chapter 6, then, is a recent addition. The case it proposes rests on a comparison between the kinds of institutions and powers Canadian aboriginal peoples advocate for themselves and those which are now in place to accommodate ethnonational political rights in such liberal-democracies as Belgium, Switzerland and Canada (to the extent that it exists with respect to the French fact). The case clearly shows that the specific propositions advanced by organizations representing most aboriginal nations are consistent with solutions already in operation in these countries. Hence, the realization of these proposals should pose no threat to the underlying values of liberal-democracy, even as they are practised in Canada.

Still, I am including the above argument with some hesitancy. The comparison seems to work in that it fits the facts as I understand them. But, as is true of the comparison between Canadian aboriginal peoples and those in other nation-states, the comparison I advocate raises important problems that need to be addressed. Two of these deserve special mention. The first is that to many, including this author, the system of liberal-democratic values upon which the Canadian polity rests is itself repleat with shortcomings that ultimately will require changes. The second is that in raising the analogy with Quebec, the argument begs to include an evaluation of the objective utility of the powers provided in Confederation to (attempt to) accommodate the French fact. However, I will not discuss them in the text. My reason is simple. The aboriginal nations are proposing a solution that seems to conform to existing constitutional arrangements and liberal-democratic ideals. Perhaps, ultimately, this solution will prove inadequate and further changes will be required. At the moment, however, the striking fact is that the aboriginal nations do not even have the special powers of self-government now accorded to the French segment. The central aim of this book is to develop an argument that will help overcome resistance to entrenching even this moderate degree of recognition, rather than one that anticipates concerns left unresolved after such recognition has been affirmed.

I wish to thank the Boreal Institute of the University of Alberta for providing me with a grant to undertake this research, and the university itself for providing a half-year study leave and partial course relief to complete the research and writing of this volume. I would like also to thank the many individuals who have assisted me. Of these, I will name only a few. Among the researchers were Shirleen Smith, Janie Ravenhurst, Kimball Morris, Howard Kirkby, Donna Lea Hawley, Rene Gadacz and Becky Cole-Will. Among the readers from whom I sought comments were Richard Price, Peter Milroy, Roger McDonnell, Lynda Lange, Michael Jackson, L.C. Green, John Foster, Harvey Feit, Billy Erasmus, Olive Dickason, Tom Andrews, Frances Abele and, especially, Gurston Dacks. Their comments all helped me to clarify and improve my effort. My thanks also to Sonia Kuryliw Paine for her diligence in editing the manuscript.

I wish to acknowledge the fact that the journal *Recherches Amérindiennes au Québec* published a French version of my chapter on aboriginal rights and the law.

1

INTRODUCTION: A PROBLEM DEFINED

> The existing aboriginal and treaty rights of the aboriginal peoples of Canada are hereby recognized and affirmed.
>
> In this act, "aboriginal peoples of Canada" includes the Indian, Inuit and Metis peoples of Canada.

With these words, contained in Section 35 of the Constitution Act, 1982, the Canadian state expressly acknowledges for the first time that there are "aboriginal people" and "aboriginal rights." For this reason alone, it is a singular moment in the history of this country.

What are the implications for Canada of the inclusion of Section 35 in the constitution? Little can be stated with authority at this time. The problem is simple: although all parties agreed to put "aboriginal rights" into the Act, there was no consensus regarding its meaning. Rather, as the constitution explicitly states, this meaning is to emerge through further dialogue and discourse. To this end, a conference was convened, attended by the prime minister, the ten provincial premiers and native representatives, to discuss among other items "the identification and definition of the rights of those peoples to be included in the Constitution of Canada (Section 37[2])." This conference took place in March 1983, and resulted only in an agreement to continue the discussions at further conferences to be held over the next five years.

However, these discussions did identify one central area of concern about the meaning of aboriginal rights as advocated by government and aboriginal representatives, respectively; namely, whether or not the definition of aboriginal rights included "special" political rights such as the right to self-determination for aboriginal peoples. This question is so basic that, in my view, it must be resolved before agreement can be reached on a definition and before the implications of the inclusion of the clause can be fruitfully examined.

This book is intended as a contribution to this process. To this end, it is divided into two major sections. The first focusses on definitions and provides a detailed account of the meaning of the phrase "aboriginal rights" as it is used by the two main actors: the Canadian state and the aboriginal peoples. The second part is devoted to an examination of the means by which the question of "political rights," which emerges from this discussion, can be resolved.

The purpose of this chapter is to introduce the fundamental concepts contained in Section 35(1) of the constitution cited above. These can be reduced to two primary terms: "aboriginal peoples" and "existing aboriginal rights." On the basis of this discussion, I shall provide a provisional definition of the potential scope of the clause "the existing aboriginal rights of the aboriginal peoples" to be used as a basis for examining the various views of its meaning, which follow.

ABORIGINAL PEOPLES

In Section 35(2) of the constitution, the phrase "aboriginal peoples of Canada" includes "the Indian, Inuit and Metis Peoples of Canada." Although the phrase "aboriginal peoples" is found in the constitution, it is not the one most commonly used to designate the collectivity of Indian, Inuit and Metis peoples; rather, "native people" or "native peoples" is used. According to the 1981 census, 491,460 individuals or about 2 per cent of the Canadian population identified themselves as members of this collectivity. Of this number, 367,810 individuals identified themselves as "Indian," 98,260 as "Metis" and another 25,370 as "Inuit." Further, it should be noted that native peoples are spread fairly evenly throughout the southern part of the country, averaging no more than 7 per cent of the total population in any one province. In the North, however, this proportion rises to 17 per cent in the Yukon and over 58 per cent in the Northwest Territories.

It can be assumed that the census produced reasonably accurate aggregate figures for Inuit and Indian peoples; the same cannot be said for "Metis." One important reason for this conclusion can be found in the census questionnaire itself, where the question asked is: "To which ethnic group did you or your ancestors belong on first coming to this continent?"

Difficulties of interpretation would be encountered when native persons answered this question, and, in fact, the census form separates their answers from the others by specifying a sub-category, "Native Peoples," under which Indian, Inuit and Metis appear. The difficulty is more acute for Metis people in that, as the census explanation itself states, they are generally considered "descendants of the unions of Natives and non-Natives" (Statistics Canada, 1981:7). Thus it is possible that a number of Metis may have responded to the question by referring to the non-native aspect of their ancestry.

This concern, and others, have led some groups that represent native peoples to challenge the accuracy of the census figures. Thus, for example, the Native Council of Canada, in its report to the First Ministers' Conference of March 1983 (entitled "Analysis Disputes

Figures on Natives"), reminds readers that "estimates for total Native population appearing between 1971 and 1980 have ranged from a low of 491,460 (census) to a high of 3,000,000" (Appendix A).

I find the criticisms valid and agree that the number of native people represented in the census is too low. The question is the magnitude of the error. In examining various statistics, reproduced in the Native Council of Canada document and elsewhere (Frideres 1983), I rely primarily on those provided by the Secretary of State, which indicate a possible range in numbers of native people between roughly 750,000 to 930,000. Taking the average of the two figures, I would then reckon a total of roughly 840,000.

The largest portion of this increase of 350,000 over the census figures, it is assumed, belong to the category of "Metis" or those native people of mixed ancestry. Thus, on the basis of the Secretary of State figures, native people would comprise about 3.5 per cent of the total population. This would make them the fourth-largest ancestral-origin group in the country, falling in behind the British, French and German.

In everyday speech, an Indian, according to Webster's Third New International Dictionary*, means "a member of any of the aboriginal peoples of the Western hemisphere, except usually the Eskimo (or Inuit)" and, it might be added in the Canadian context, the "Metis." The word also has a precise legal definition, which is contained in the Indian Act: "a person who pursuant to this Act is registered as an Indian or is entitled to be registered as an Indian (Section 2[1])." In general, such persons are those whose ancestors were defined as Indians at the time of the first Indian Act in 1868. However, there are important exceptions. Included as Indians under the terms of this Act are, for example, non-Indians who are the wives of registered Indians. Excluded are persons who in other respects conform to the terms of the Act but who, for example, by deciding to vote prior to 1960, declared themselves (and their descendants) to be non-Indians, those who voluntarily enfranchise, and those who through some indirect action caused the loss of their Indian status. In this latter category, perhaps the best-known are Indian women (and their descendants) who, by marrying persons not defined as registered Indians, fall outside the domain of the Act and thus lose their status.

In order to differentiate between these categories of "Indian," government has divided Indians into two sub-groups: "status

---

*All material from Webster's Third New International Dictionary used by permission. Copyright © 1981 by Merriam-Webster Inc., publisher of the Merriam-Webster® Dictionaries.

Indians" refers to those persons who are registered under the Act; and "non-status Indians" are those who have lost, or as the government phrases it, *"have not maintained* their rights as status Indians" (Statistics Canada n.d.:7). Government, although using a separate verbal designation for non-status Indians, has tended to place this group, administratively, into the same category as "Metis"—a category that, at least until the Constitution Act of 1982, did not have "special" rights as aboriginal people.

It is presumed here that the term Indian, as it is applied in the aboriginal rights clause of the constitution, is not used in the sense defined in the Indian Act, but rather in the commonly known sense defined above. Therefore, I followed this sense of the term in the statistics cited above and lumped together the totals of status (290,000) and non-status (80,000) Indians together to arrive at the total number of "Indians" (370,000), as derived from the census.

Used in this sense, "Indian" is a collective term that designates a wide variety of groups and individuals who have many different languages, cultures and histories. The breadth of this diversity is reflected, for example, in the recent name change of the national organization which represents status Indians in Canada. Once called the National Indian Brotherhood, it is now the Assembly of First Nations, symbolizing the notion of a confederation of distinct national entities. Following this view, I believe it would be useful to conceptualize the term Indian, as it appears in the constitution, as equivalent in applicability to "European," and the various collectivities that comprise its constituent members as analogous, in terms of their inter-group differences, to the various nations of Europe.

The term Inuit, perhaps because it is not yet confounded by legal or administrative descriptions, is easier to define. The word has recently replaced "Eskimo" (which has a negative connotation to Inuit because of its Algonquian meaning of "eaters of raw flesh"). According to Webster's Third New International Dictionary, Inuit are "a group of people of northern Canada, Greenland, Alaska and eastern Siberia (or) a member of such a group." It is presumed that this is the meaning given to the word as it appears in the constitution. As such, it designates a collectivity characterized by a higher degree of similarity in language, culture and history than does "Indian." Perhaps the closest analogy, in terms of homogeneity, might be the regional European grouping of nations designated as "Scandinavians."

"Metis" is the third word in the series. Dictionary definitions of this term all seem to emphasize the racial characteristics of the individuals who belong to the group and exclude any concept of cultural collectivities to which the individuals could belong. Typical is the definition of "Metis" in Webster's Third New International Dictionary: "one that is of mixed blood; half-breed; specifically, one of French and Indian ancestry." Although one can be certain that the term does incorporate such individuals, in my view such a definition is incomplete. There are groups, such as the Alberta Metis colonies represented by the Federation of Metis Settlements, that exist as social collectivities that are Metis in their linguistic, cultural and historical characters. Aside from the use of the term for self-designation and the racial origin of certain of its members, the key attributes of Metis collectivities revolve around the fact that they are hybrids who have developed out of the mixture of cultural elements drawn from both Indian national entities and those of primarily French, but also English, settlers. As a collectivity, Metis groups range widely in their cultural patterns and include, in some instances, groupings that are not readily separable from ways of life of certain "Indian" nations, on the one hand, or patterns of European settlement, on the other. In my view, common usage does include such entities within the concept of "Metis." It is therefore presumed that the framers of the constitution did not intend to exclude this idea from the meaning of "the Indian, Inuit and Metis peoples of Canada," but rather that, in this instance at least, the dictionary definitions lag significantly behind the common meaning of the term as it is entrenched in the constitution.

"Aboriginal peoples," then, has three related meanings. First, it refers to those contemporary societies that trace their historical ancestry, at least in part, to those societies that existed in Canada prior to European contact and settlement. Second, it means members of such societies. Finally, it refers to persons who, although not currently members of such societies, can trace their biological ancestry through at least one line to individuals who belonged to them.

EXISTING ABORIGINAL RIGHTS

The aim of this section is to provide a working definition of "aboriginal rights" that should help guide the discussion to follow. For this purpose, it is best to begin by examining, separately, the meaning of (1) aboriginal, (2) rights, (3) aboriginal rights and (4) existing, and then to attempt a derivation of the phrase as a whole.

"Aboriginal" is defined in the Oxford English Dictionary (1933) as "dwelling in any country before the arrival of the later (European) colonists." As an example of its usage, the dictionary cites Edmund Burke's 1788 phrase "this aboriginal people of India." It is assumed that this is the sense intended in the constitution's phrase "aboriginal peoples of Canada."

I have found no description of "right" or "rights" that summarizes a consensus view on all aspects of its meaning, and I will not attempt one here. Rather, I shall try to pinpoint what I understand to be the meaning of "rights," as applied to "aboriginal rights" in the constitution. To this end, the most important fact to note is that there are certain rights that are expressly acknowledged in the constitution. This means that it is unnecessary to argue whether or not these rights exist, despite the fact that the state does not acknowledge them. The question, then, is to what does "rights" refer in the constitution?

In principle, there are many kinds of rights that could be the subject of the constitutional definition. However, an examination of the usage in Canada limits these to two possibilities. The first refers to rights of self-government and self-determination, such as the "power to participate directly in government" (Black 1968:1487) normally associated with the existence of a viable political society. These kinds of rights are often referred to as "constitutional" rights, and are sometimes seen as an aspect of human rights. As Sutton says for the Dene (1977: 50): "aboriginal peoples have significant, internationally recognized political or human rights, including the right to enjoyment of culture and the right to survival and self-determination." The second possibility refers to a property right in land and/or a right to hunt, fish and trap. According to Cumming and Mickenberg (1972: 13), "Aboriginal rights are those property rights which inure to Native peoples by virtue of their occupation of certain lands from time immemorial."

To which of these possibilities does the constitution subscribe? Aboriginal peoples would maintain, to *both*. Government, however, traditionally argued, at least in its rhetoric, that there were no aboriginal rights of either sort. This view is changing. In the 1970s representatives of government (mainly at the federal level) accepted the idea that matters respecting property, but not political rights, could be introduced into a definition.[1] More recently, there is evidence to indicate that some government representatives (again mostly federal) are prepared to consider that "special" political rights also be included in the constitutional meaning of this term.

Does the constitution require these changes in attitude on the part of government? Or, to the contrary, does it deny native peoples special political rights? No one knows, for as I stated at the outset, the document itself is mute on the subject of what the term means. Indeed, it is hoped by all parties that the constitutional dialogue now taking place between representatives of the aboriginal nations and the provincial and federal levels of government will act to resolve these matters in a mutually satisfactory way so that an acceptable definition can be introduced into the constitution.

Clearly, it is not possible at this time to provide a definition of "rights" as it appears in "aboriginal rights" with any degree of certainty, much less finality. Therefore, for the purposes of the present discussion, I assume that the word, as it appears in the constitution, refers to (1) matters of ownership such as property rights, land title, or rights to use the land and its resources for certain purposes; and/or (2) a corpus of human or constitutional rights, which can include the right to political self-determination for the aboriginal peoples of Canada. In this book, although information will be provided on both aspects of this definition, the focus will be on matters pertaining to the possible inclusion of "special" political rights within the scope of "aboriginal rights" as it appears in the constitution.

The term aboriginal rights is qualified by "existing." The presumed meaning of this word as it is intended in the constitution is best understood by examining the reasons for its introduction. In January 1981, the three federal parties agreed to the inclusion of a clause (Section 34) which stated: "the aboriginal and treaty rights of the aboriginal people of Canada are hereby recognized and affirmed." Then, in early November, after the First Ministers' Conference, it was announced that the section had been deleted at the request of certain provincial premiers.

Among the objections raised, two, vocalized mainly by Premier Peter Lougheed of Alberta, stand out. "Premier Lougheed told the Alberta Legislature . . . he objected to Section 34 because it did not define the rights being entrenched" (*Edmonton Journal*, Nov. 11, 1981). The second pertained to a fear that if the set of rights referred to was not fixed with respect to a particular moment in history, "new rights" could be continually added to it, some of which, in the premier's view, might have a negative impact on the rights of other citizens. In an effort to bound the corpus of "aboriginal rights" in this manner, Premier Lougheed proposed the following change in the definition of aboriginal rights: "The aboriginal and treaty rights of the aboriginal people in Canada, *as those rights exist prior to coming into force of this part*, are affirmed" (original emphasis) (*Edmonton Journal*, Nov. 12, 1981).

In late November of 1981, after much lobbying by aboriginal peoples, their organizations and other Canadians, a section on aboriginal rights was re-introduced into the constitution through an all-party agreement. However, two changes were made. The first, which apparently was intended to accommodate concerns about "vagueness," was the call for a First Ministers' Conference to define "aboriginal rights." The second was the insertion of the qualifier "existing" to "aboriginal rights." This, it can only be assumed, was done in order to ameliorate the concern about fixing the corpus of aboriginal rights, articulated by Premier Lougheed. However, the phrase conveys other meanings, and it is possible that it might be defined differently. Nonetheless, for the moment it is fair to assume that the intention of "existing" is to ensure that in future the corpus of "aboriginal rights" is not changed from that which was already in place at the time of patriation.[2]

Thus, "existing aboriginal rights" refers to that "corpus of rights which derive from the fact that aboriginal peoples were present (dwelled) in Canada prior to the arrival of the European colonists as they were bounded into a fixed set at the time of the patriation of the Canadian Constitution." The phrase "are recognized and affirmed," then, places a constraint on the Parliament of Canada, the provincial legislative assemblies and other members of the body politic to act in accord with the acknowledgement of these rights, regardless of their political will to do otherwise.[3]

CONCLUSIONS AND SUMMARY OF CHAPTERS

The Constitution of Canada establishes two points: there is a corpus of rights called "aboriginal rights," and at least some of these rights (most likely those deemed to exist at the time of patriation) are recognized and affirmed by the sovereign. Thus the central point in dispute is not the acknowledgement by the Canadian state of the concept of "aboriginal rights." Rather, it is what content ought to be included within the meaning of the phrase, and in particular—at least with respect to the following discussion—whether it includes the political right of self-determination.

The recognition, in principle, of aboriginal rights is a point to underscore, for it represents a reversal in state policy of the greatest magnitude. In 1969, after a long period of debate (see Weaver 1981), the federal government announced a "new" policy based on the necessity of rapidly assimilating native peoples into Canadian society. This was to be accomplished through "termination," a policy which was "designed to eradicate all special Indian rights in the near future" (*ibid.*: 197). The document that announced the policy direction, the "Statement of the Government of Canada on Indian Policy, 1969," explained the rationale behind termination in this way (DIAND 1969: 5, 8):

> The policies proposed recognize the simple reality that the separate legal status of Indians and the policies which have flowed from it have kept the Indian people apart from and behind other Canadians.

Hence, the new

> policy rests upon the fundamental rights of the Indian people to full and equal participation in the cultural, social, economic and political life of Canada.

> To argue against this right is to argue *for* discrimination, isolation and separation. No Canadian should be excluded from participation in community life, and none should expect to withdraw and still enjoy the benefits that flow to those who participate. (original emphasis)

Regarding property claims related to aboriginal rights (such as an aboriginal claim to land), the policy paper succinctly stated (*ibid.*: 11): "These are so general and undefined that it is not realistic to think of them as specific claims capable of remedy except through a policy and program that will end injustice to Indians as members of the Canadian community. This is the policy that the government is proposing for discussion." In short, it was a policy that denied the existence of aboriginal rights itself.

This position was further underlined in a speech given by Prime Minister Trudeau in August 1969 after the announcement of the White Paper. In an address in Vancouver, he stated, "we say we won't recognize aboriginal rights." (Cumming and Mickenberg 1972: 331-32). He went on:

> ... aboriginal rights, this really means saying, "we were here before you. You came and you took the land from us and perhaps you cheated us by giving us some worthless things in return for vast expanses of land and we want you to re-open this question. We want you to preserve our aboriginal rights and to restore them to us." And our answer—it may not be the right one and may not be one which is accepted but it will be up to all of you people to make your minds up and to choose for or against it and to discuss with the Indians—our answer is "no."

It is a position he justified by concluding:

> If we think of restoring aboriginal rights to the Indians well what about the French who were defeated at the Plains of Abraham? Shouldn't we restore rights to them? And what about though the Acadians who were deported—shouldn't we compensate for this? And what about the Japanese Canadians who were so badly treated at the end or during the last war? What can we do to redeem the past? I can only say as President Kennedy said when he was asked about what he would do to compensate for the injustice that the Negroes had received in American society. We will be just in our time. This is all we can do. We must be just today.

Perhaps the clearest evidence of the magnitude of the entrenchment of the phrase aboriginal rights is illustrated in Prime Minister

Trudeau's opening statement (1983: 2) at the March 1983 Constitutional Conference: "Canada's constitutional process cannot be held to be fulfilled if the (aboriginal) peoples, whose ancestors have been here the longest, find that their particular rights are not adequately reflected or protected in the Constitution."

Singular among the reasons for this about-face was the lobbying effort of the aboriginal peoples themselves in opposing and convincing other Canadians to oppose a policy that they found totally unacceptable (Weaver 1981: 198 f). Other factors during the 1970s, such as the Mackenzie Valley Pipeline hearings, also played an important role. Of these, perhaps none was more important to government than the decision made by the Canadian courts concerning the legal basis for aboriginal rights. This is a topic that will be taken up in some detail in Chapter 4.

In short, on the basis of these developments, the aboriginal peoples of Canada are closer than at any point in recent history to having their political and property rights explicitly acknowledged by the Canadian state. It is a situation that is symbolized most crucially by the affirmation and recognition of their "aboriginal rights" in the constitution. Yet, there is still some distance to go, for, although the phrase does appear in the constitution, until it is given a substantive definition, the value of its appearance is only symbolic.

In the chapters that follow, I intend to explore issues that relate to the possible realization of "special" political rights for aboriginal peoples and, in particular, the right to a distinct form of self-government within Confederation. Although the idea of special political rights was rejected by the state in recent years, its realization, in my view, now appears stalled mainly because of a reluctance of governments to enter into what appears to be an uncharted field. My objective, as I stated in the Prologue, is to try to encourage the overcoming of this reluctance. To this end, I have decided to organize the book as follows:

I begin, in Chapter 2, by discussing some aspects of the cultural basis out of which arose the political rights claims advanced by representatives of aboriginal nations. In Chapter 3, I present the argument made by these representatives at the March 1983 First Ministers' Conference in defence of their claims to political rights, including the right to self-government. This is followed, in Chapters 4 and 5, by an examination of how two organs of the state—the courts and the federal government—have viewed aboriginal rights over the years. The discussion emphasizes questions of property and social rights, and shows that court decisions and government statements over the years could be interpreted in a manner consistent with the possibility of the inclusion of special political rights for native peoples. This is followed, in Chapter 6, by an analysis that should indicate that certain fundamental fears about exploring the possibility of interpreting "aboriginal rights" as political rights are unfounded. Finally, Chapter 7 is a detailed exposition of the propositions for self-government put forward by various aboriginal nations. It shows that the proposals represent a conciliatory act intended to foster the entrenchment of their rights in a manner consistent with principles of liberal-democratic rule.

NOTES

1. See Flanagan (1983 a) for a view that uses the quotation from Cumming and Mickenberg cited in the text to suggest that Metis do not have aboriginal property rights.
2. For a full discussion of the possible implications of the use of "existing" in the constitutional section on aboriginal rights, see Slattery (1983).
3. A common, if disputed, view of the nature of "rights" is contained in Webster's Dictionary. Here it is said that a "right" is simply "something to which one has a just claim." This view focusses upon the idea that rights are *individual claims*. This is one of many possible approaches (Benditt 1982). One approach that is useful in understanding the meaning of "constitutional rights" is contained in the work of Richard Claude (1976), who having focussed on the historical origin of the concept within Western political tradition, describes these rights less as a claim by individuals than as an imposition of "lawfulness" placed upon a sovereign's actions by his subjects. Claude illustrates this perspective with reference to the English Civil War of 1642-49 (*ibid.*: 13). This war, it must be recalled, concerned King Charles' attempts to govern without Parliament from 1629 to 1640. In 1637, Sir John Hampden was prosecuted for refusing to pay a tax. The question at issue during the ensuing trial, according to Claude, was whether "the power to arrest and detain him (was) exercisable at the king's pleasure, or was it subject to rules laid down by law?" (*ibid.*). The courts sided with the king, for they agreed he had the authority to act outside of Parliament. In 1640, Parliament disputed this authority and, as Claude says, the English Civil War that followed centred on "the question of whether the king was bound by the law" (*ibid.*). As is well known to students of English history, Parliament won the war and therefore 'proved' the answer to that question to be "yes." This view was acceded to in 1689 by William and Mary, who signed a document that is now known as the English Bill of Rights.

   The language of the Bill of Rights itself provides further confirmation of Claude's orientation, for the clauses are clearly directed at constraining actions of the sovereign than at protecting the rights of individuals (as implied by Webster's definition).

   Finally, support can be found for Claude's view from a seemingly surprising source: the American Bill of Rights. This document, which is perceived to be the keystone for entrenching individual freedom, actually does so in the case of religion, speech and the press, in the same kind of language as appears in the English Bill of Rights. That is, rather than expound on the rights of individuals and the justice of their claims, the First Amendment to the American Constitution (1949: 282) states: "*Congress shall make no law* respecting an establishment of religion, or prohibiting the free exercise thereof; or abridging the freedom of speech or of the press; or of the right of people peaceably to assemble and to petition the government for a redress of grievances."

In sum, a constitutional right is perceived not as a shield which, like a just claim, arms or protects the individual from the actions of others, especially from the state. Rather, it is more like a cage that constrains the sovereign, be this an individual or a parliament, to act within a known framework of lawfulness, even when it has the will to act otherwise. Thus, a constitutional right is a collective possession, won by the body politic, that forces the sovereign to become a socialized and, in that sense, no more and no less than an equal member of the body politic.

2
CONTEMPORARY NATIVE LIFE: IMAGES AND REALITIES

INTRODUCTION

Most Canadians, as a survey undertaken by Ponting and Gibbins (1980: 67-94) attests, are conversant with the fact that descendants of the aboriginal peoples of this country face a litany of social, psychological and economic problems unparalleled in any other segment of Canadian society. Indeed, as the survey shows, it is mainly the presence of such problems that comes to mind when the majority of Canadians are asked to differentiate Canadian Indians from the general population (*ibid.*: 76).[1] Thus, I venture to say that most Canadians would agree with the notion that despite differences in geography, culture and legal distinctions, "Native Canadians do share one common feature: across Canada, they lead marginal lives, characterized by poverty and dependence. Indeed, many people argue that Natives are members of a culture of poverty" (Frideres 1983: 185).

There is no doubt but that this image appropriately reflects one reality faced by aboriginal society. But does it tell the whole story? Are, in fact, native society and culture indistinguishable from the Canadian mainstream, except for certain "curious" cultural practices and the extremeness of certain endemic material, social and psychological pathologies? Is contemporary native society truly just a culture of poverty?

The answer to all these questions, in my view, is "no". In this chapter I wish to present an image of native peoples that counters that held by most Canadians. I focus not on the very real problems faced by aboriginal peoples, but rather on those cultural features that remain in place and that, even after the long period of contact, still shape these societies in a manner distinct from the Canadian mainstream.

I wish to make it explicit at the outset that the perspective advanced here is not intended to deny that serious problems exist, or to assert that nothing has changed. Nor is this chapter written as a *justification* for the acknowledgement of "special" political rights for aboriginal peoples. Rather, my analysis is intended to balance the partial image that now rests in the public mind with a different perspective and through such a process provide a better factual and conceptual framework against which current proposals can be assessed.

Obviously, the best way to accomplish such an objective would be to record the present way of life for as many native societies as exist. However, such a task would be well beyond constraints of space and the ability of this writer. A second alternative would be to survey findings made by others; indeed, a number of detailed studies have been published recently upon which one could draw.[2] A third approach would be to focus on one specific situation to illustrate the general theme. I have chosen the latter course, focussing on one case study, that of the Dene of the Northwest Territories, and utilizing information about other groups only to elaborate particular points. I chose the Dene because it is the society with which I am most familiar and because the Dene have developed a proposal for self-government, called Denendeh, that, I believe, is relevant to the discussion on self-determination.

Dene society is quite complex. It exists in various forms and covers a geographical region that extends over 500,000 square miles. Hence, to deal with the Dene situation effectively requires further constraints. Rather than discuss many aspects of Dene life, I shall concentrate on the economy—primarily because I am convinced it is harder to imagine continuity here than in other areas (such as religion, language and worldview). Furthermore, since the Dene economy varies from one region to another, I shall concentrate on one region—the Slavey (it is the region I know best, and comparative studies indicate that the Slavey economic pattern holds for other regions as well).[3] In addition, because my intent is to illustrate patterning over time, the discussion includes both the contemporary situation and historical antecedents. As a result, detailed coverage of the contemporary economy will be less than might otherwise be expected.

In sum, what follows is a discussion of the economy of the Dene who live in the Slavey region, as their economy has evolved over time. It is intended to illustrate that dynamics existing outside the framework of the Canadian mainstream are still operative in native society.

THE DENE

The Dene (pronounced de-nay in English) is an aboriginal nation whose homeland encompasses an area of over 460,000 square miles in Western Canada's sub-Arctic and Arctic regions. The term Dene itself means "people" in a number of their own languages, and is used extensively today as a term of self-designation by members of the nation. The nation is made up of a large number of regional groupings, some of whom speak different but often mutually understandable languages. Among these groupings are the Hare, Dogrib, Slavey, Kutchin and Chipeweyan. Collectively, the Dene are known in the anthropological literature as Northern Athapaskan-speaking Indians.

The Slavey grouping inhabit the area stretching from Lake Athabasca (Alberta) to the south, then northward along the Athabasca, Slave, Liard, Hay and Mackenzie rivers to a point near the Mackenzie Delta. It is bounded in the west by the Rocky Mountains and in the east by the northern extension of great plains, known as the barren grounds. The region is dominated by lakes, rivers and other waterways cutting through low-lying plains. The forest cover is mainly jack pine, birch and spruce. Depending on how far north the location is, the land remains frozen and covered with ice and snow for up to seven months each year. Summers, though as short as three months in places, are surprisingly warm, with sunshine for most of the day. The two dominant seasons are separated by brief transition periods known as "freeze-up" (when the land becomes frozen) and "breakup" (when the ice on the rivers, lakes and land melts). The region is rich in fish resources, as well as small game such as beaver, rabbits, marten and lynx. Moose and woodland caribou are also found extensively. Breakup and freeze-up are times when migratory birds pass through the region in large numbers, and summer provides an intense growing season for a wide variety of berries such as rosehips, strawberries, raspberries and "saskatoons," as well as other plants.

The economy[4] of the Slavey prior to first contact with Europeans in 1789 was based entirely upon the consumption of locally produced and finished materials. The primary unit of consumption and production was the local band, which consisted of approximately twenty to thirty individuals related by kinship ties. In the winter, these local groups camped along the shores of the larger lakes, where small game and fish—the major dietary staples—were found in most constant supply. In the summer, a number of bands would assemble together for a time at one of the more productive lakeside spots (probably in areas of fish runs). Such an assembly, known as a regional band, consisted of about 150 people. Among the Slavey, the total population in this period is estimated at 1,250 individuals, comprising eight regional bands.

The division of labour within a local band was organized by age and sex. Adult men were responsible primarily for hunting big game and for fishing; women, children and elderly men for small game and berries. Women's tasks included, among other jobs, the making of clothing out of such materials as moosehide and rabbit skins. The productive technology used to capture game was mainly snaring or trapping; even moose were taken by this means. Given such a technology, it is apparent that the harvesting of resources was a labour-intensive activity that required both individual skill and much cooperation.

Circulation of goods within local bands was accomplished on the basis of reciprocity or mutual sharing. Generally speaking, the evidence indicates that all members participated equally in the good fortune of the hunters, and all suffered equally when their luck turned bad. Although distribution within the group was generally informal, there was some degree of formal recognition given to the individual hunter through the retention of certain parts of the animal for the use of his family. In this way, individual hunting skill was acknowledged, but not at the expense of the well-being of the group as a whole.

In good times, it appeared that there was little circulation of goods between local bands. However, occasionally the local region harvested by one or more of these groups was found wanting. Usually, this did not indicate a general regional scarcity, but rather a shift in distribution of certain game, and this meant that other bands in the Slavey region were likely experiencing some surplus. At such times, the problem for the Slavey became how to create a balance between those bands with a surplus and those with insufficient resources. The answer, given the nature of the technology and the kinship system, as reported by earlier travellers, was not to move the goods to the bands, but rather to move people from areas of scarcity to those of plenty. As a result, the concept of mutual sharing was extended both in principle and in fact to the regional band as a whole.

In the 200 years since first contact, the Dene of the Slavey region have been introduced to much European-based technology, institutions and values. A few examples will suffice to illustrate the extent of this penetration. Through the fur trade in the nineteenth century the Dene were offered and adopted a wide variety of trade items. Of these, among the most important included flour, tea, tobacco and sugar, which soon became dietary staples; repeating rifles and steel traps, introduced in the late 1800s, which helped to make hunting and trapping more efficient; and, by the turn of the twentieth century, cloth and clothing of Western manufacture. Missionaries of both the Roman Catholic and Anglican faiths established their first missions in the region in 1858, and within fifty years had converted, at least nominally, all the Slaveys to one of these faiths.

Government, as well, has had a major impact on Slavey life. Although it established a presence in the latter part of the nineteenth century, it was not until after the Second World War that it became a major force. Since 1945, the government has introduced family-allowance and old-age-pension benefits, which, along with welfare, have provided major sources of non-labour-based cash to the Slavey economy. It introduced compulsory education programs and established permanent schools in many settlements in the region; it constructed housing and nursing stations; it introduced such improvements as water delivery and electricity in the communities; and provided much of wage employment for Slaveys in the region. All of these 'benefits' have been accepted by the Slavey people.

When one looks at any Slavey community today, the results of these adoptions are clearly visible. People live in towns serviced by water delivery and electricity rather than in the bush, dwell in permanent houses and not in tents, attend Christian churches, send their children to public school, speak fluent English, accept welfare among other cash benefits from government, and often work for wages—sometimes on a full-time basis. It is apparent from such facts that Slavey society in general and the economy in particular have shifted greatly, in certain respects, from its pre-contact form.

The Slavey way of life is no longer identical to that which existed prior to contact. Along with the above changes have come a litany of social, economic and psychological problems that have become typical of contemporary native societies. Among these are a higher rate of alcoholism than the majority of the Slavey would desire; an economy that generates less cash income than is necessary to fulfill material needs without greater reliance on welfare payments than is charac- teristic of the national average; and poor-quality houses that often do not have running water or indoor toilet facilities.

For this evidence, then, one could conclude that Slavey society today is characterized by a lifestyle that is distinguishable from the Canadian mainstream, primarily by its societal pathologies. But would such an assessment be completely accurate? The answer, as the discussion below should attest, is no. There are other significant differences.

One of the most clearly observed manifestations of change in the Slavey economy is found in the wholesale adoption of Western tech- nology and goods. One significant example is Slavey reliance on store- bought foods. Observing a Slavey child eating a candy bar or drinking a soft drink, one might be tempted to conclude that the Slavey diet is comparable to that of the average Canadian child—or at least to one who is poor. Yet, although some Slavey families do rely heavily on store-bought foods, generally, bush foods such as those harvested in the pre-contact period (and prepared in the traditional manner) still provide significant nutrition in their diet. One measure of the con- tinued reliance on these foods is provided by government statistics. According to 1968 government figures,—a time after people had moved into town,—regional country food production (excluding rabbits and fish which, although dietary staples, were not included in the statistics) exceeded 180 pounds of meat (edible weight) per capita. This meant that Slaveys were able to sustain their meat needs at a level equal to that of the average Canadian without making one purchase from the store (Asch 1976).

But research has shown this figure to be low. According to Rushforth, who surveyed country food production in Fort Franklin, members of that community harvested (excluding small game such as rabbit and beaver which are often eaten) over 150,000 pounds of meat (edible weight) or over 400 pounds per capita. One portion of this production was used to fulfill human subsistence requirements and another, mainly fish, the needs of sled dogs. According to his estimates, one-third of the total food requirements for humans and animals was met through country food production: an amount that saved the community approximately $200,000, which otherwise would have been spent to purchase store foods imported from southern Canada (Rushforth 1977: 40). Another study by Ken Bodden (1981: 116) shows parallel results for the Slavey community of Fort Resolution on the south shore of Great Slave Lake. His statistics indicate that income from country food and fur production used to fill domestic needs (as opposed to sale) accounted for 35.6 per cent of total income in 1975-76 and about 27.5 per cent in 1977-78. The report of the Mackenzie Valley Pipeline Inquiry (Berger 1977: Chapter 2), which examines the socioeconomic and other impacts of a proposed gas pipeline in the region, confirms the general accuracy of the specific findings made by Rushforth and Bodden. According to this report, in the mid-1970s, Dene, in their homeland as a whole, generated approximately 34 per cent of their total income through bush-food and fur-collection activities (for domestic consumption). To paraphrase Usher (1976: 119), who upon citing statistics concerning Inuit country food production, commented: If these are "poor" people, they are surely the only ones in Canada who regularly go to bed with their bellies full from meat provided from their own larders.

The ability to sustain such a significant level of country food production is based largely on the use of Western technology such as the rifle, the skidoo and the steel trap. It is therefore ironic that many people consider the adoption of such items as symbolizing the abandonment of native traditions. Often, given the contemporary situation, it is only through the use of this frequently expensive technology that native people are able to pursue their traditional land-based subsistence activities. As Derek Smith pointed out with respect to the native people in the Mackenzie Delta (1975: iii):

> More people are engaged in casual labour and are living in settlements in improved housing. But this does not mean that the land and its resources have become less significant for native people. There is less fishing, since there are fewer dogs to feed, but there is more hunting (and more effective hunting) for meat for human consumption. Our 1965-1967 data on the use of land resources estimated native peoples' reliance on these resources in terms of cash equivalent values. This

showed that land activities were very significant. There are other more powerful ways of estimating the relationship of the land. For example, a quick re-examination of our 1965-1967 data shows that *over 75%* of the protein demand of native people was met by land resources. An equally quick calculation based on more recent figures showed that this *scale of reliance on land resources is essentially the same.* (original emphasis)

This statement applies equally to most Dene communities.

There are obvious changes, as well, in the institutional and value structures on which Slavey economic life is organized. One, of singular importance, has taken place in the primary unit of production and consumption. While the people lived in the bush, the local band was the primary unit of production and consumption, even into the mid-twentieth century. But the move into communities since that time has not led to the band's rapid demise, nor has the band been replaced by the nuclear family, as might be expected. Rather, the primary unit today is the household: a grouping that typically consists of at least three generations of family members. Furthermore, for many economic activities, this group expands to incorporate kin who normally live in other households, as, for example, is the case when cousins go to the bush to hunt and trap together. Thus, the household appears to be a compromise between the collective orientation associated with the local band form of production and the individualized, self-sufficient nuclear family organization of mainstream Canadian society.

In other respects, the household provides a locus for the continuity of many of the institutions and values associated with the traditional Slavey economy, particularly because of the direct link between the household and participation in activities associated with bush production. Each household tends to remain self-sufficient in country food production, and to accomplish this end is organized so that bush-related activities remain a central pivot for all family members. Typically, Slavey men, regardless of age, and even full-time jobs, regularly harvest big game, fur bearing animals and fish, even when this means returning to the sites of traditional bush camps, for long periods, without their families. Other members of the household maintain their roles in the traditional division of labour, hunting small game, gathering berries and processing the raw materials harvested by the men. In exploiting bush resources, members of the household, despite the introduction of rifles and snowmobiles that allow the possibility of individual production, still use cooperative and collective forms of labour; for example, when herding caribou or moose toward a particular kill-site. This possibility is extended on a regular basis to multiple households and even to communities through participation in communal hunts. Finally, despite the introduction of freezers, which would allow game to be kept for long periods, surpluses are not hoarded by individual households. Rather, as is traditional, when a household's luck is good, the 'fortune' is generally shared with other households in the community on the basis of mutual reciprocity.

In sum, although significant changes have taken place, resulting in obvious problems, it would be wrong to conclude that they indicate the demise of an economic formation that is distinctly Slavey. Rather, to be accurate one must describe contemporary Slavey economy as a mix of innovation and continuity that allows for the maintenance of traditional Slavey institutions and values, as well as bush products. Similarly, I would argue that an analysis of kinship, ideology or any other factor would provide convincing evidence that, despite long and sustained contact and the adoption of non-traditional lifestyles and values, Slavey society is still distinct from the way of life of non-native Canadians, regardless of their economic background. In short, despite what appears to be obvious evidence, it would be highly inappropriate to reduce Slavey society to a "culture of poverty."

SOME COMPARISONS

Detailed research into the economies of such diverse native societies as the Inuit of Labrador (Usher 1980), the Cree (Feit 1982) and the Montagnais-Naskapi (Tanner 1979) of James Bay, Quebec, and the Beaver (Brody 1981) and Shuswap (Asch 1981) of British Columbia confirm these observations. On the one hand, important new technologies have been adopted, some groups have been employed in wage labour to a significant degree, and there have been cases of serious economic and social problems. But, on the other hand, despite these factors, many contemporary native societies retain strong elements of autonomous cultural systems. As Feit suggests for the James Bay Cree (1982: 384 f):

> . . . production and sharing of (country) food, and economic interdependence among Cree themselves, remain central to Cree economic and social life. Although hunting and wage employment provide roughly equal contributions in dollar value to the total economic outputs at a community level, hunting is the more valued activity, it is the more stable activity and it remains most closely and reticulately linked to the local social and cultural structures that are central to Cree life and that the communities clearly desire to maintain.

In sum, despite certain outward appearances, nations such as the ones cited above cannot be characterized as cultures of poverty, nor can it be said that their members are merely assimilated poor people who happen to be of aboriginal ancestry.

The cultures cited thus far do share one important feature in common: they are all associated with the production of bush resources. It is therefore fair to ask if hunting and trapping are essential to the maintenance of viable cultural traditions among contemporary native peoples. One point is clear: it appears to be more certain that aboriginal peoples will retain significant autonomy in their way of life if such activities are practised than if they are not. For example, although the Shuswap Indians of Alkali Lake in the interior of British Columbia live near urban centres and often have a full-time job, their cultural traditions remain distinct from those of other residents in the region. A key factor that accounts for this phenomenon is hunting.

Obviously, one reason that hunting persists is economic. Alkali Lake people, like many others (native and non-native alike), find game less expensive and more tasty than store-bought meat. However, the main reason is found in the institutions and values associated with success in hunting itself. For instance, the act of hunting provides the context for the culturally appropriate way to transmit values about the land and the Shuswap's place upon it. The food obtained in this way enables young band members to learn production techniques such as preparing meat and dressing hides. Most important, in my view, is that the distribution of country food functions as a rationale to continue the custom of traditional sharing among band members. This institution, which characterizes many contemporary native societies, is, even among the more urbanized Shuswap, crucial in linking band members into a cohesive unit based on traditions and values that are unlike those found in the Canadian mainstream. In short, it is in the reciprocity associated with successful hunting that, along with institutions related to kinship and ideology, one finds evidence of the continuity of an autonomous way of life. Indeed, I would argue that it is the association of institutions such as reciprocity with hunting, rather than the production of country food itself, that is the crucial factor that accounts for autonomy.

Given that this is so, clearly, hunting itself is essential mainly in that it provides the best opportunity for traditional values to be practised within contemporary settings. However, other settings can be used, and I am certain that production of any sort can be used in the same way. The difficulty is that often they are not. Yet, this is not to say that when hunting is lost so are traditional institutions and values.

There are instances, even in cities, where this is not the case. For example, kinship relations and institutionalized reciprocity are used to link individuals who no longer participate in bush activities to traditional lifeways. Often this takes place through sharing between city-

and country-dwellers who belong to the same nation and thus can act to link urban native persons to their traditional setting and values. However, reciprocity can also be used to create cultural networks among urban native peoples themselves. Often these exchanges involve sharing Western technical expertise (such as how to repair a car or truck), staging of native events (such as pow-wows), or teaching traditional skills (such as handicraft-making, dancing or story-telling). When effective, these act to bind individuals together more tightly than is usual among members of the Canadian mainstream, and this network often allows the transmission of cultural information that traditionally took place in different settings. Finally, when reciprocity is bound up with such mechanisms as Native Friendship Centres, which provide foci for larger social networks to develop, the opportunity for the maintenance of distinct cultural systems increases. Thus, despite the possibility of extreme poverty in an economic sense, urban native peoples often have the institutional resources necessary to retain their identity as people who live within, but do not wish to be assimilated into, the Canadian cultural mainstream. As such, it is impossible to state with certainty that even urban native people with no direct links "back to the land" have lost contact with an autonomous past to become transformed into members of a "culture of poverty."

CONCLUSIONS

It is clear that the image Canadians have of aboriginal peoples does not conform well to reality. Why is this so? In my view, the answer lies in the fact that the average Canadian is not confronted with sufficient information to discourage a stereotyped image.

Stereotypes are created out of partial images and tend to dominate perception primarily when there are few facts with which to make judgements. Thus, as Levi-Strauss has illustrated (1969: 46), indigenous societies, perhaps because of the paleness of the European skin colour in comparison to their own, frequently stereotyped the explorers who first contacted them as ghosts, gods or ancestors. In one celebrated case, Cortes, the Spanish conqueror of Mexico, was mistaken by the Aztecs for Quetzalcoatl, an Aztec culture-hero of light skin colour, recently transformed into a god. A confused Montezuma, then king of the Aztecs, openly welcomed Cortes into the city, which he immediately conquered.[5] Given the consequences of this stereotype, there can be little doubt but that the Aztecs quickly replaced this image of Cortes with one which took into account facts more relevant to their circumstances than his skin colour.

Early European perceptions about aboriginal peoples are also full of stereotypes. For example, early in the history of contact, there was a serious debate among the colonists as to whether the human-like creatures found in the New World were in fact people, for there is no mention of their existence or ancestry in our charter myth—the Bible. It was a stereotype that was overcome only after the Pope declared, in 1512, that the inhabitants of the New World were in fact human (MacGowan and Hester 1962: 12).

However, although Papal authority managed to dispel this stereotype, it was quickly replaced by another and then yet another. But what is even more unique than the persistence of stereotyping is the degree of consistency in the manner in which the images are formed. Thus, the gulf between "our humanity" and "their non-humanity" characteristic of the pre-1512 view was replaced in the seventeenth and eighteenth centuries with a distinction between the original inhabitants of the New World, who were construed to live in a "state of nature," and the creators of the image, who were seen to be living in a "state of society." This image, in turn, has been translated in the nineteenth and twentieth centuries into one that contrasts the "primitive" state of native peoples and their society with the "civilization" of Europeans. In short, whatever the terms of the comparison, Canadians, from first contact to the present, have maintained a single stereotyped view of native peoples: they are distinguished by their inferior and undesirable qualities.

Curiously, anthropologists, despite our training and our avowed scepticism about accepting revealed "truths" (at least those that originate in Western thought), have not been immune from the naïve adoption of this theme in our models. As Upton, an historian, rightly notes (1973: 54), it was with the rise of anthropological interest in cultural and physiological classification of human beings in the early nineteenth century that the British Reform Movement found the intellectual basis upon which their evolutionary comparisons were based. Even in the more recent past, anthropological models, such as the one developed in acculturation theory to explain the course of change under conditions of contact, have echoed similar perceptions. Typical is the statement by Murphy and Steward made in a seminal article on acculturation (1956): "When the people of an unstratified native society barter wild products found in extensive distribution and obtained through individual effort, the structure of the native culture will be destroyed." In other words, the acculturation stereotype seems to suggest that the process of contact between a "primitive" and an "advanced" society will lead inevitably to the former's demise.[6]

In my view, the perception of contemporary native society as a culture of poverty is merely another manifestation of the acculturation version of the stereotype. In this type, a perceived evolutionary opposition, which is bridged in the post-contact era by acculturation, is replaced by one based on relative wealth and social harmony which, presumably, must be bridged in the future through the development of the more "primitive" society. In essence, then, it replaces the attributes of primitiveness, sub-humanity, or pre-societal condition of native society with one that images poverty and other deprivations. At the same time, it suggests the idea, as intimated by Murphy and Steward, that the inevitable consequence of the process has been the destruction of an autonomous aboriginal entity.

But, as the evidence in this chapter indicates, the stereotyped image of contemporary native peoples is inaccurate. The fact that these societies exhibit continuities that clearly link their present institutions, values and other aspects of their lifestyle to a history that reaches back to an aboriginal past establishes firmly that native societies continue to survive, at least in some significant respects, as autonomous entities. In not taking this reality into consideration the conventional perception has produced an image of contemporary native peoples as inaccurate as Montezuma's image of Cortes.

But what is a realistic image? In the first place it is one that acknowledges that aboriginal societies today are more than just cultures of poverty. There is no need to recount the course of colonization to accept that its introduction of new populations, technologies, values and institutions into previously autonomous lifeways is unparallelled in recorded history. Given the massive scale of this process over the past four centuries, it would be no wonder if, as the conventional image portrays, aboriginal cultural patterns had been completely destroyed. Yet, they withstood the impact. One may well ask whether the lifeways of Europeans and their descendants could have survived as well, if at all, under the same historical conditions.[7] In short, given the evidence of continued autonomy, native peoples ought to be perceived not as failures, with undesirable qualities, but rather as successful survivors worthy of admiration.

The realization that success, at least as much as failure, is appropriate to the image of contemporary native society has started to impinge upon the consciousness of Canadians. Employers in the North who once viewed Dene and Inuit peoples as merely cultures of poverty have begun to make wage labour more attractive to native workers by providing regular periods of time off for bush-production activities. Government, too, through processes such as land claims negotiations and the Berger Commission, has come to realize the same lesson and is starting to plan policy on the assumption that aboriginal societies will retain their cultural integrity (see Chapter 5). Until recently, Canadians in the south were not presented with the kind of information that could alter their stereotyped image of contemporary native society. Today, however, with constitutional talks under way, along with proposals for aboriginal self-government, a whole new dimension of data is fast becoming available. It is just possible that with this new data in hand, Canadians will begin to lose their false image of native peoples, which has blinded them to a full understanding of the facts.

NOTES

1. Although the most often-cited single response was "cultural differences," an overwhelming majority of responses (79%) referred to factors such as "education level," which would indicate the existence of "problems" characterizing native societies.
2. See list of references in Appendix K.
3. Helm (1981) provides a number of examples from adjacent Dene groups that confirm this assertion.
4. The economy of the Slavey prior to first European contact is known primarily through the archaeological record, the writings of early explorers and traders and local environmental conditions. The account presented here is based on one consensus interpretation of this body of data. However, other interpretations exist (e.g., Krech 1980; Yerbury 1980). Elsewhere (Asch 1980, 1982), I have explained my reasons for rejecting these.
5. I am grateful to my son, Seth, whose social studies report provided the data for this illustration.
6. It would be unjust as well as inaccurate to give the impression that acculturation theory is not constantly under review. Elsewhere (Asch 1983), I discussed the reappraisals taking place in the analysis of post-contact history among Athapaskanists. Revisions are also taking place in other ethnographic regions. I chose anthropological examples primarily for the purpose of illustrating the extreme position among the colonists' descendants, and not to suggest unanimity in the acceptance of its tenets.
7. Descendants of the colonists imagine that our ancestors discovered a New World. In fact, it would be more accurate to suggest that we discovered a new landscape in which to place our existing world. In fact, it was the indigenous peoples who had a new world to discover and to deal with upon the arrival of the Europeans.

3

ABORIGINAL RIGHTS: THE VIEW
OF THE ABORIGINAL PEOPLES

Aboriginal peoples have long maintained that they have "special" rights that differentiate them from other Canadians. These rights, which include property rights (such as title to unceded lands), rights to hunt, fish and trap on traditional lands and political rights (such as the right to self-government), are presently called "aboriginal rights." In this chapter, I shall describe the current position of aboriginal organizations with respect to political rights, only.[1] Although there are different ways to conceptualize the basis of the legitimacy of special property and use rights (see the chapter on Aboriginal Rights and the Law), it is apparent that, ultimately, aboriginal peoples would perceive these as flowing from the same source as their political rights. In this sense, then, while focussing on political rights, the discussion will bear some relationship to the position taken by aboriginal peoples on the issue of aboriginal rights as a whole.

Two preliminary questions must be posed at the outset of this task. The first is whether it is possible for a non-native person to understand the meaning of "aboriginal rights" well enough to express it accurately. The second is whether a consensus view of the meaning of aboriginal rights can be discovered, for there is no single official body from which one can elicit the 'official' position of the aboriginal nations as a whole. The first concern will be dealt with during the course of the chapter. The second I shall address now.

The central difficulty with respect to this question is the large number of groups that have an independent standing to speak on behalf of a legitimate aboriginal constituency. Since the constitution defines aboriginal peoples as consisting of three distinct groups (Indian, Inuit and Metis), they are represented by at least four national organizations: the Assembly of First Nations (AFN), which represents status Indians; the Native Council of Canada (NCC), which speaks for non-status Indians and Metis; the Metis National Council (MNC), which also speaks for Metis; and the Inuit Committee on National Issues (ICNI), which represents the Canadian Inuit. Further, each of these national organizations is a coalition of smaller ones. The AFN, for instance, includes the provincial organizations that represent status Indians in each of the ten provinces and two territories. Each of these, in turn, is composed of sub-regional and local groupings such as tribes and bands. Each unit within the AFN, from the individual band to the national organization itself, has a legitimate right to put forward a stance on aboriginal rights independent of any other body. When the situation within the AFN is multiplied by the same situation within the Metis and Inuit organizations, the scope of the difficulty in deciding which group is representative becomes obvious. To further complicate matters, there is a second national Indian organization. Called the Coalition of First Nations, it has taken positions on the resolution of specific issues of self-government that are at variance with the stand taken by the Assembly of First Nations.

What is difficult to do under the circumstances, then, is to decide which group(s) is representative. Fortunately, this does not have to be done here, for although the various aboriginal peoples speak with different voices, my analysis of the documentation on aboriginal rights indicates virtual unanimity concerning the meaning of the principle, and, despite some exceptions (such as the position of the Coalition of First Nations—see Chapter 7), a high degree of consensus with respect to how the principle is to be carried out in practice. It is, furthermore, a point of view that has been maintained for over fifty years.

The current position of aboriginal nations on their rights was stated by the AFN, NCC, MNC and ICNI at the March 1983 First Ministers' Conference on Aboriginal Rights. It is this meeting that will be the focus of attention below. Although I shall concentrate on the words of the spokespersons for the four national organizations, what they state is consistent with virtually every other statement to which the reader might wish to refer.

THE DEFINITION OF ABORIGINAL RIGHTS

The nature of the consensus view of aboriginal rights is not hard to identify. For the Inuit, according to John Amagoalik, co-chairperson of the Inuit Committee on National Issues:

> Our position is that aboriginal rights, aboriginal title to land, water and sea ice flows from aboriginal rights and all rights to practise our customs and traditions, to retain and develop our languages and cultures, and the rights to self-government, all these things flow from the fact that we have aboriginal rights.
> . . . In our view, aboriginal rights can also be seen as human rights, because these are the things that we need to continue to survive as a distinct peoples in Canada. (Canada 1983a: 130)

For the Metis, Clem Chartier of the Metis National Council, asserted:

> What we feel is that aboriginal title or aboriginal right is the right to collective ownership of land, water, resources, both renewable and non-renewable. It is a right to self-government, a right to govern yourselves with your own institutions, whichever way you want your institutions to run; the right to language, to culture, the right to basically practice your own religion and customs, the right to hunt, trap and fish and gather are certainly part of that, but it is not all of it. (Canada 1983a: 134)

These views are replicated, as well, in the draft proposal to amend the constitution presented by National Chief David Ahenakew on behalf of the Assembly of First Nations. Included within this draft are specific provisions that would guarantee autonomous cultural and economic status for aboriginal peoples, protect historically acquired lands and, most crucially, entrench the following political rights:

1. The right of the First Nations to their own self-identity, including the right to determine their own citizenship and forms of government.

2. The right to determine their own institutions.

3. The right of their governments to make laws and to govern their members and the affairs of their people . . .

4. . . . Their right to exemption from any direct or indirect taxation levied by other governments.

5. The right to move freely within their traditional lands regardless of territorial, provincial, or international boundaries. (Assembly of First Nations 1983: 5.5)

An examination of the content of these and other statements presented at the conference indicates that the most significant concepts in the minds of the spokespersons pertain to a political jurisdiction that includes a land base. For example, David Ahenakew argues that central to the position of the AFN is the notion of some measure of Indian "sovereignty" and "jurisdiction" (1983: 8). He states: "we are . . . asserting that Indian governments have jurisdiction over Indians, Indian lands and resources" (*ibid.*: 9). Echoing this sentiment, Mr. Clem Chartier asserts that "the purpose of our participation in this conference is to entrench in the Constitution the right of the Metis people to a land base and self-government" (Canada 1983a: 30). The same view recurs in statements made by every native organization that has put forward a position on aboriginal rights, from the band to the national levels.

A consensus view is also expressed with respect to the conceptual basis upon which these assertions are justified. Singularly important are two firmly held convictions. The first is that aboriginal rights is founded on the fact of "original" sovereignty. That is, as Georges Erasmus, president of the Dene Nation, put it at the Constitutional Conference (Canada 1983b: 43): "We are talking about the title that our people had prior to contact with the European people and obviously . . . the rights we also had at the first contact was full sovereignty." The second is the notion that the continuing existence of those rights that are founded on this original sovereignty have not been extinguished through the subsequent occupation of Canada by settlers from Europe and other parts of the world. It is a proposition explained in contrasting but equally relevant manners by two aboriginal spokespersons from British Columbia. For James Gosnell, chief of the British Columbia region of the AFN, the position derives from an ontological premise based on the principle of the "gift from God," which is reminiscent of the traditional basis for the assertion of sovereignty under a European feudal polity. He says (Canada 1983a: 114 f):

> It has always been our belief, Mr. Chairman, that when God created this whole world he gave pieces of land to all races of people throughout this world, the Chinese people, Germans and you name them, including Indians. So at one time our land was this whole continent right from the tip of South America to the North Pole . . .

> It has always been our belief that God gave us the land . . . and we say that no one can take our title away except He who gave it to us to begin with.[2]

For Bill Wilson of the Native Council of Canada, the principle of original sovereignty is linked to the principle of liberation that motivated Canadian involvement in the Second World War. As he states (Canada 1983a: 122):

> When the German forces occupied France, did the French people believe they didn't own the country? I sincerely doubt that there was one French person in France during the war that ever had the belief that France belonged to Germany, which is why, of course, they struggled with our assistance to liberate their country and once again take it back for themselves.

Later, he adds (p. 124):

> So what we say is we have title and that is why we are talking
> to you about aboriginal rights, but we are not talking English
> Common Law definitions . . . international law definitions
> that have been interpreted and re-interpreted and sometimes
> extinguished by conquest and ceding treaties and other
> agreements like that. We are talking about the feeling that is
> inside . . . all of us as Metis, Indian and Inuit people that this
> country belongs to us.

In sum, then, aboriginal rights can be described as encompassing a broad range of economic, social, cultural and political rights. Of these, it appears that the notion of a land base within a separate political jurisdiction is fundamental. These rights flow, first of all, from the fact that the aboriginal peoples were in sovereign occupation of Canada at the time of contact, and secondly from the assertion that their legitimacy and continued existence has not been extinguished by the subsequent occupation of Canada by immigrants.

That this is the consensus view, there can be no doubt. The question is, whether such a notion is comprehensible within, and compatible with, a non-native conceptual framework?

At first blush, it would appear that it may not even be possible to discover the answer. The concern pertains to an ability to communicate cross-culturally the understanding of the meaning of this term as it is conceptualized by native peoples within their cultures. It is a concern which was put most forcefully by Bill Wilson when he stated (Canada 1983a: 128): "My whole point [is] that we must stop viewing [aboriginal rights] from the point of view of the dominant society if we are ever going to understand what the Indian people, the Inuit people and the Metis want." The first issue, then, is whether there is a means of understanding this concept from the native point of view.

At some level, this is a problem that cannot be completely resolved, at least not without in-depth training and detailed study of a particular culture. The reason for this is simple. Concepts do not exist in a vacuum, but rather are understood in relation to other concepts. Therefore, in order to know the meaning of "aboriginal rights" as it is understood within a particular native society, it is necessary to know how it relates to other notions within that society. This matter is complicated further by the fact that the term itself may be merely an English gloss that is used for convenience' sake, but at the same time encapsulates a bundle of notions that cannot be readily translated from a native language into English. Thus, without knowing a native culture and understanding the logical structure of meaning of a particular native language in some depth and breadth, one can only hypothesize in general terms about the viewpoint held by any grouping of aboriginal peoples. That is, the best one can do is provide an interpretation that comes close to capturing the general meaning as it is understood within a native culture and language.

Such a task is made much easier if one can find an analogue from the conceptual schema used in one's own society. As the above indicates, such an orientation cannot do justice to the full sense of the concept as it is understood by native societies, but it can, I believe, provide a framework for cross-cultural understanding. The question, then, is whether there is a concept within our intellectual framework that is analogous to the notion of a peoples' right to a land base and self-government that derives from original sovereignty and remains unextinguished, even in the face of the acquisition of sovereignty by a new political authority.

At first, the answer would seem to be "no"—for a logical reason. World history has seen so much population movement and conflict over land that were a concept of ongoing rights based on original habitation to be accepted as valid, a general state of confusion in world affairs would result. This is an argument that was put most forcefully by Prime Minister Trudeau when, in a retort to Mr. Wilson and Chief Gosnell, he said (Canada 1983a: 127):

> Going back to the Creator doesn't really help very much. So He gave you title, but you know, did He draw on the land where your mountains stopped and somebody else's began . . .? God never said that the frontier of France runs along the Rhine or somewhere west of Alsace-Lorraine where the German-speaking people of France live. . . . I don't know any part of the world where history isn't constantly rewritten by migrations and immigrants and fights between countries changing frontiers and I don't think you can expect North America or the whole of the Western Hemisphere to settle things differently than they have been settled everywhere else, hopefully peacefully here.

This is a persuasive argument, and, speaking in general terms, it is this point of view and not that of the aboriginal peoples that has become adopted in the conceptual schema of the world community.

There are, however, circumstances in which the world community appears to recognize, in principle, an exception to this general proposition. One situation, alluded to by Mr. Wilson in his comment about the French under German rule in World War II, is when the inhabitants of a previously recognized country fall under the occupation of what is perceived by the world community to be a foreign power. This principle is encapsulated in the proposition respecting the territorial integrity of nation–states (United Nations 1961). A second and perhaps more appropriate circumstance pertains to the situation of colonialism, in particular that aspect of colonialism in which peoples of non-European origin came under European rule. In both kinds of circumstances, the consensus view of nation–states acknowledges that, despite the self-evident emergence of a new sovereign and even immigration, the rights of the indigenous people (be they French or African), and in particular their sovereign rights, may not be completely extinguished or eliminated—at least in principle—even by the overt act of the new sovereign. It is, I believe, to these circumstances that one must turn if one is to comprehend, through analogy, the basis of the declarations made by aboriginal spokespersons.

The general concepts within which the expression of these sentiments is legitimized within the world community's intellectual schema are "self-determination," or the "recognition of the right of all people to rule themselves" (Cranston 1966: 92), and especially that right as it is perceived to exist under the condition of "colonialism," or "the aggregate of various economic, political and social policies by which an imperial power maintains or extends its control over other areas of peoples" (*ibid.*: 17). Although these terms are not precise or obvious with regard to meaning (see, for instance, the question of the definition of "self" in self-determination),[3] it is my view that these general notions describe well the position implied in the expression "aboriginal rights."

Further evidence that this is the case can be derived by comparing the words of the aboriginal leaders cited above with the wording of a number of international accords, such as the Charter of the United Nations (Chapter XI), the Covenant of the League of Nations (Article 26) and, in particular, resolution 1514 (XV) of the United Nations General Assembly. Entitled the Declaration on the Granting of Independence to Colonial Countries and Peoples, this resolution passed without a dissenting vote in 1961. In part, the words say:

Mindful of the determination proclaimed by the peoples of the world in the Charter of the United Nations to reaffirm faith in fundamental human rights, in the dignity and worth of the human person, in the equal rights of men and women and of nations large and small and to promote social progress and better standards of life in larger freedom.

Recognizing the passionate yearning for freedom in all dependent peoples and the decisive role of such people in the enforcement of this independence.

Recognizing that the peoples of the world ardently desire the end of colonialism in all its manifestations.

Convinced that all peoples have an inalienable right to complete freedom, the exercise of this sovereignty and the integrity of this national territory.

Solemnly proclaims the necessity of bringing to a speedy and unconditional end colonialism in all its forms and manifestations;

And to this end

Declares that:

1. The subjugation of peoples to alien subjugation, domination and exploitation constitutes a denial of fundamental human rights, as contrary to the Charter of the United Nations and is an impediment to the promotion of world peace and cooperation.

   (and)

2. All peoples have the right to self-determination; by virtue of that right they freely determine their political status and freely pursue this economic, social and cultural development.

Compare this to the Dene Declaration that was passed unanimously by the Dene chiefs at a meeting in Fort Simpson in 1975:

We the Dene of the Northwest Territories insist on the right to be regarded by ourselves and the world as a nation.

Our struggle is for the recognition of the Dene Nation by the Government and people of Canada and the peoples and governments of the world . . .

The New World like other parts of the world has suffered the experience of colonialism and imperialism. Other peoples have occupied the land—often with force—and foreign governments have imposed themselves on our people. Ancient civilizations and ways of life have been destroyed.

Colonialism and imperialism is now dead or dying. Recent years have witnessed the birth of new nations or the rebirth of old nations out of the ashes of colonialism . . .

The Dene find themselves as part of a country. That country is Canada. But the Government of Canada is not the government of the Dene. These governments were not the choice of the Dene, they were imposed upon the Dene.

Although it is not clear that the United Nations had the situation of the aboriginal peoples of Canada in mind when it passed resolution 1514 (XV) and other resolutions,[4] there is evidence to suggest that, in principle, its point of view parallelled the sentiments expressed by aboriginal peoples. As well, the sentiments expressed in these documents appear to concur with the perceptions of aboriginal peoples. Hence, I would argue that an appropriate analogy exists between the two points of view.

In sum, I would assert that the notion of aboriginal rights in the perceptions of the native leaders is analogous to the right to self-determination acknowledged by the world community as applicable to peoples living under colonial regimes. Here, then, is the counter-argument to the prime minister's position. Canada in this view is not a 'normal' nation-state to which 'normal' legal processes such as those cited by the prime minister apply. Rather, Canada is seen as a colonial manifestation, that, in principle, has no more right to assert permanent sovereignty over the land mass of Canada and over its original inhabitants than did, say, the British in Kenya or the French in Indo-China.

What, then, is the implication of making such an assertion? Although the resolution of the rights of an indigenous population under colonial rule to self-determination has taken many forms, in the classical scenario it is accomplished through the establishment or re-establishment of a nation-state founded on an indigenous sovereignty. Is this what is being asserted by the aboriginal peoples in Canada? Are they, in other words, calling for the breakup of Canada?

In principle, one must accept that, according to the logic of their position, they would be justified in demanding such an action. What is abundantly clear, however, is that their proposals eschew such a solution. That is, no proposition from the four national organizations calls for the severance of the aboriginal population from the Canadian state or for the formation of an independent, autonomous nation-state or nation-states based on an indigenous sovereignty. Rather, the solution is always seen as realizable within the context of Confederation. Thus, the Metis National Council states (1983a: 1):

> The purpose of our participation in this Conference is to entrench in the Constitution the rights of the Metis people to a land base and self-government. We believe the realization of these rights is essential to the preservation and development of our aboriginal nationality within the Canadian federation.

And Chief Ahenakew of the AFN states (1983: 5):

> I ask . . . that no one misinterpret our positions, strongly held,

> or our words, no matter how strongly spoken to mean that
> we are separatists—seeking to divide Canada and assert the
> status of foreign nations. . . . We are committed to strength-
> ening and building Canada—not to dismantling it.

That this is a consensus view of long standing can perhaps best be seen
by referring to the conclusion of the strongly worded Dene Declaration cited above: "What we seek . . . is independence and self-determination within the country of Canada."

How, then, do the aboriginal peoples propose to resolve their right
to self-determination? Here, native organizations differ significantly,
especially with respect to specifics (see Chapter 7). Nonetheless, they
agree on two fundamental points. First, all assert that the objective is
limited to insuring that the aboriginal peoples continue to survive and
develop as distinct nations; and second, that this necessitates a
restructuring of the Canadian political system in a manner that will
guarantee aboriginal people the exclusive legislative authority deemed
"necessary for (our) survival and development as a distinct people (or
peoples)" (Metis National Council 1983a: 1).

In general, all native organizations agree that to achieve this end
requires jurisdiction over aboriginal lands and over those aspects of
the lifestyle of aboriginal peoples that influence directly economic,
linguistic, cultural, educational and other related matters. They specifically exclude aspects that are of less direct consequence; for example,
the AFN suggests that their demands do not include the establishment
of "our own armies and our own foreign relations" (Ahenakew 1983:9).

The national native organizations propose that the creation of new
institutions of responsible self-government is the key solution. However, there is a wide divergence in viewpoint concerning the shape
these institutions should take. Two positions tabled at the conference
serve as examples. The AFN envisages the replacement of the present
binary division of powers between the federal and provincial levels
with one based on a tripartite set of jurisdictions. These would incorporate the present federal and provincial areas with a new one that
would be known as "Indian Governments." The latter would have
responsibility over matters of direct concern to the survival and
development of the aboriginal nations. They would consist of band
governments with an overarching jurisdiction responsible for issues
common to the various nations. It appears to envisage no alteration to
the current jurisdiction or composition of the federal and provincial
jurisdictions.

The result of this proposal would be the creation of three equal
governments, each with sovereignty within its own jurisdiction; that
is, as the AFN proposal suggests (Ahenakew 1983: 10):

> Indian governments will have exclusive sovereignty and jurisdiction over matters coming within our powers; the Federal Government will continue to have exclusive sovereignty and jurisdiction over matters coming within its powers; and the Provincial Governments will continue to have sovereignty and jurisdiction over matters coming within their domain. Relations between our Governments and other orders of government in Canada will be altered only by mutual agreement, as is the case today between the Provinces and the Federal Government.

The second proposal was put forward jointly by the Native Council of Canada and the Metis National Council in separate position papers. It advocates both the establishment of new institutions of native self-government and changes in the present federal Parliament and provincial legislatures. With respect to this latter aspect, the proposal calls for the replacement of the present system of membership in these bodies with one that, in addition to the present system, would add a guaranteed number of seats reserved exclusively for the descendants of the aboriginal peoples. The proposal is unclear as to the nature of the new native jurisdictions. Whereas it calls for the establishment of new institutions of self-government, it does not make explicit whether these jurisdictions would be co-equal to that of the federal and provincial governments, as is advocated in the AFN proposal, or whether they would have a level of authority junior to the present structures. There is evidence to support both views. For example, the latter position holds first of all because the interpretation was not firmly rejected by the representatives of the Metis and non-status Indians at the Constitutional Conference, and second because this is the most probable justification for the insistence on guaranteed seats in the federal and provincial legislatures (that is, special seats should have special responsibilities). However, other evidence, such as the statement made by the Manitoba Metis Association, asserts (Manitoba Metis Rights Assembly 1983: 11): "We do not want token seats (in Parliament and the Manitoba legislature) as an alternative to real self-government," and as such lends weight to the former interpretation.

Regardless which interpretation proves correct, it seems clear that the position held jointly by the MNC and the NCC does not differ in fundamental philosophy from that proposed by the AFN. In effect, both propositions call for an identical kind of transformation of the Canadian political system from its present form to one that explicitly recognizes, within its political structure, the existence of an autonomous aboriginal entity. The difference really is only in emphasis and in the degree to which this recognition is to be acknowledged within the political structure of the Canadian nation-state. Thus, it follows that from the point of view of the native organizations, although the assertion of aboriginal rights does not call for the breakup of Canada, it does demand changes to its present institutional structure.[6]

SUMMARY AND CONCLUSION

In my understanding, the nub of the position of the native organizations is that aboriginal peoples have the right to maintain ways of life that are distinct from those of recent immigrants to Canada. These ways of life are not to be interpreted as ethnic in the sense of a Canadian mosaic, but rather as a composite of autonomous systems that integrates languages, economies, social organizations, political organizations, religions and other values into a total culture. Central to the ongoing viability of these is a land base and self-government.

The right to preserve and develop such autonomous systems in Canada is perceived to derive, in part, from the manifest failure of the current programs designed to establish viable lifeways for the majority of the aboriginal population. However, at the core, it arises from a vision of Canada as a colonial manifestation and from the perception of aboriginal peoples as "colonized" nations that, like those indigenous populations on other continents, have an inherent right to assert their self-determination and control over their own affairs.[5] It is a goal that is perceived to be attainable within the context of Confederation.

In this view, then, the inclusion of a clause on aboriginal rights in the constitution symbolizes the recognition of a legitimate claim to political rights analogous to those found in colonial situations. Seen in this light, the proposals for self-government must be considered moderate indeed, for they call for a resolution without disrupting the continuity of the Canadian state. Short of denying any right to political self-determination, the proposals represent the least possible position from the point of view of aboriginal peoples.

Nevertheless, such a view of aboriginal rights is not widely shared by Canadians, or even by representatives of government. Thus I am certain that no matter how moderate the solutions appear to be, there will be some who would continue to object to the principle itself. Still, as I intend to show in the following two chapters, the Canadian state has recently advanced positions that are more favourable to the aboriginal peoples' position on political rights. Indeed, as mentioned in Chapter 1, objections raised to the entrenchment of these rights today, as a general rule, rely much more on practical concerns or considerations of a possible negative impact on liberal-democratic institutions (of which more in Chapter 6), than they do on simple rejections of the stand itself. The key to this change is a shift in the manner in which aboriginal peoples are conceptualized at the time of first contact. It is a change that receives its first important acknowledgement by the Canadian state in court decisions concerning the legitimacy of the claims to aboriginal title to lands as yet unceded to the Crown—a subject to which I turn in the following chapter.

NOTES

1. For a succinct statement on property and use rights, see National Indian Brotherhood (1973: 42-44).
2. Chief Gosnell's words echo the description of the origin of aboriginal sovereignty found in Louis Riel's final trial speech, when he said (Flanagan 1983b: 254):

> In England, in France, the French and the English have lands, the first was in England, they were the owners of the soil and they transmitted to generations. Now, by the soil they have had their start as a nation. Who starts the nations? The very one who creates them, God. God is the master of the universe, our planet is land, and the nation and the tribes are members of His family, and as a good father, he gives a portion of his lands to that nation, to that tribe, to everyone, that is his heritage, that is his share of the inheritance, of the people, or nation or tribe. Now, here is a nation strong as it may be, it has its inheritance from God. When they have crowded their country because they had no room to stay anymore at home, it does not give them the right to come and take the share of all the tribes besides them. . . . This is the principle God cannot create a tribe without locating it.

3. An excellent summary of competing definitions of "self" in the twentieth century is contained in Ofvatey-Kodjoe (1977: 28-38). In his view, three theories have been dominant: "national determinism," in which the nation that is the "self" is an ethnic community; the "plebicite," in which the self is "a group of people with a common subjective attachment to the same state"; and "national equality," which sees the "self" as based on a mix of "a common territory and nationalistic outlook" (p. 36). A fourth theory, "national-cultural autonomy," is mentioned but not developed. It is a position that was raised by the Austrian socialists, but was never adopted as state policy (ibid.: 36).

Ofvatey-Kodjoe suggests that of the three dominant theories two have been seen to have serious defects that make them unpopular from the perspective of developing an international community. The problem with the national-equality theory can be reduced to a concern over precision in applicability, especially in difficult cases such as those that might arise if two nations co-exist within the same state. The problem with the national-determinism theory is that it appears to be anti-democratic in the sense that it does not allow people to choose their sovereignty through popular will, and, as well, suffers from its association with the conceptual basis of nationalism under the German Nazi regime. In his opinion, it is the plebicite theory that the international community favours in defining "self." It is seen, in my readings, to be a commonly held view by experts.

The primary implication of this theory is that it is only the majority of the population that has the right to self-determination within a national entity. As Higgins suggests (1963: 104, 105):

> . . . self-determination refers to the rights of the majority within a general accepted political unit to the exercise of power. In other words, it is necessary to start with stable boundaries and permit political change within them. . . . If, then, the rights of self-determination is the right of the majority within an accepted political unit to exercise power, there can be no such thing as self-determination for the Nagas. The Nagas live within the political unit of India and do not constitute the majority therein.

The idea propounded by Higgins concerning majority rule could have an important consequence for Canadian aboriginal people. Some authorities would follow her interpretation and argue that, like the Naga of India, the native people of Canada, as a minority of the total population within a recognized nation-state, have no special political rights under provisions of United Nations declarations. The idea of majority rule within recognized jurisdictions (but of a subnational order) is developed in Chapters 6 and 7. A further discussion of this topic within the context of United Nations provisions follows in note 4 of this chapter.

4. The problem is that the aboriginal peoples of Canada are unlike the indigenous populations on other continents: they are a numerical minority, and they are contained within a recognized nation-state. Thus, by some interpretations, they would be considered a minority population, and, as the plebicite theory (see note 3 above) suggests, they would not have a right to self-determination (for a discussion of ethnonational politics of such minorities, see Conner, 1973). There is evidence to suggest that at least some nation-states would prefer, on practical and political grounds, to see this interpretation adopted in principle. However, no resolution does so. Rather, the documents appease the concerns of these nation-states by relying on peripheral considerations to exclude indigenous groups from the effects of the responsibilities of the administrative powers. Thus, for example, resolution 1514 (XV), in interpreting which self-governing territories had to have their development toward self-government reported upon, stated that it was a self-evident proposition only when the "colony" was ethnically and/or culturally distinct *and* geographically separate from the administrating power.

In short, the issue is debatable. Clearly, the United Nations has much trouble in dealing with this issue, perhaps because most nation-states have minorities within their national borders that could use principles such as those contained in resolution 1514 (XV) to demand self-determination. Yet, the United Nations has not denied, in principle, that at least some of these groups could have the same right to self-determination as is proclaimed by resolution 1514 (XV). For a detailed discussion on this point, see Bennett (1978).

5. For a detailed academic discussion in support of this view, see Barsh and Henderson (1982) and Sanders (1983a, 1983b). For a counter-position, see Green (1983).

6. The Dene and the Inuit of the Northwest Territories have made proposals for self-government that would not necessitate the creation of a new level of government. However, their position also requires institutional rearrangement. The strongest advocate of this proposition at the First Ministers' Conference was the ICNI.

4

The Discovery of Aboriginal Rights in the Law[1]

A basic principle of English legal tradition, applied to the British colonies, is that the indigenous citizens of newly acquired dominions do not automatically lose their property or civil rights. The rationale behind this idea is quite simple: you should not lose title to your house merely because a new ruler has asserted sovereignty in your country. The same notion holds for civil rights. Until the new sovereign has declared them to be of no effect, one must presume that they continue to exist. For example, at the time of the United States invasion of Grenada in November 1983, Commonwealth legal experts expressed concern about actions taken by American authorities to counter laws passed by the military council. As the *Globe and Mail* put it (5 November 1983), "Although it may be argued that the military council ceased to exist with the success of the invading U.S. Marines, legal experts in the Caribbean and Canada say that under constitutional law the existing People's Laws remain in force until they are abolished by the 'supreme authority'."

In this case, the principle could be negated by pointing to the cooperation of the governor-general of Grenada (who acts as head of state) with the marines and, perhaps, by reference to the invocation of a mutual-aid treaty. Nevertheless, the principle still stands. The new ruler may pass general legislation (that is, laws that do not speak directly to the question of the original inhabitants' rights) that have the effect of diminishing the rights of the original inhabitants; however, until the new ruler expressly extinguishes these rights through an intentional act (such as a law revoking them), they still stand. With regard to property rights, it is generally held that any act that expropriates such matters as title to land ought to include provisions for compensation for value lost. In other words, "The general rule of law in expropriation cases is and has long been that compensation is given and any statute providing for expropriation without compensation must be expressed in the clearest and most unequivocal terms" (Challies 1963: 77). Thus it appears that, regardless of the merits of the case based on the concept of decolonization (see Chapter 3), the aboriginal peoples of Canada should retain, under English law, those property rights they possessed prior to colonization that have not been expressly extinguished by specific legislation and/or for which compensation has not been paid.

Any difficulty the aboriginal peoples may have had in establishing these aboriginal rights, then, does not stem from any defect in the principles of English law. Rather, the problem lies in the failure to recognize that this legal principle ought to be applied to the aboriginal peoples of Canada. I begin this chapter by illustrating the nature of this problem by reference to legal interpretations made in different historical eras, and I close with a more detailed examination of recent court decisions that seem to indicate a fundamental change in the traditional way of thinking.

ENGLISH COLONIAL LAW AND ETHNOCENTRISM

At the heart of the matter is ethnocentrism. This form of bias favours what is familiar and denegrates what is different. Thus, it has always been easier for British courts to recognize ongoing legal rights in newly acquired territories where the local inhabitants had traditions and values similar to their own. With colonial expansion, the British acquired territories whose inhabitants had traditions, values and a lifestyle quite different from their own. In these situations, the British courts typically failed to address these differences in a relativistic sense, but rather, following the dictum of ethnocentrism, perceived them as indications of inferiority. Thus, speaking broadly, throughout the colonial period the question of acknowledgement of rights that existed prior to contact deferred to a very different one: Did the colonized peoples even have the kind of society that could contain rights that could be recognized by a civilized court of law? If not, then they had no case to make.

Since the law is founded on the application of reason and logic, the courts developed a 'test' to determine the answer to this question. But since the ideology within which this test was administered was ethnocentrically biased, so was the instrument itself. In the Elizabethan era, this test hinged on religious considerations. Christians, it was argued, might have such rights; infidels, as non-Christians, never could. The reasoning behind this position was put most succinctly in Calvin's case in 1608 when the court said (Calvin's Case 1608: 398):*

> And upon this ground there is a diversity between a conquest
> of a kingdom of a Christian King, and the conquest of a king-
> dom of an infidel; for if a King come to a Christian kingdom
> by conquest, seeing that he hath *vitoe et necis potestatem*, he may

---

*Most references in this chapter are cited separately under *Cases and Statutes* in the bibliography.

at his pleasure alter and change the laws of that kingdom: but until he doth make an alteration of those laws the ancient laws of that kingdom remain. But if a Christian King should conquer a kingdom of an infidel, and bring them under his subjection, there *ipso facto* the laws of the infidels are abrogated, for that they be not only against Christianity, but against the law of God and of nature. . . .

The most recent example of this test is found in a 1919 decision made by the Judicial Committee of the Privy Council (then the supreme tribunal for the Empire). In a case involving the indigenous people of Southern Rhodesia, Lord Sumner, speaking for this Court, stated (Southern Rhodesia 1919: 233):

The estimation of the rights of aboriginal tribes is always inherently difficult. Some tribes are so low in the scale of social organization that their usages and conceptions of rights and duties are not to be reconciled with the institutions or the ideas of civilized society. Such a gulf cannot be bridged. . . . On the other hand, there are indigenous peoples whose legal conceptions, though differently developed, are hardly less precise than our own. When once they have studied and understood they are no less enforceable than rights arising under English law.

What is clear, then, is that although the parameters of comparison had changed, the underlying view, that there could be a test based on ethnocentric criteria, had not. "Civilization" had merely replaced "Christian" as the fundamental basis for the establishment of the rights of indigenous peoples. And, it is crucial to point out that the very test described above is still used by the courts of this country to determine whether or not the aboriginal rights of a particular nation can be recognized.

THE ACQUISITION OF A NEW TERRITORY

The use of such ethnocentric notions can have strong repercussions for the descendants of aboriginal peoples. A crucial illustration of this problem is found in the theory by which new dominions can be acquired. There are, following Slattery (1979), four ways in which this can occur: (1) by conquest or the military subjugation of a territory, over which the ruler clearly expresses the desire to assume sovereignty on a permanent basis; (2) by cession or the formal transfer of a territory (by a treaty, for example) from one independent political unit to another; (3) by annexation or the assertion of sovereignty over another political entity without military action or treaty; and (4) by

settlement or the acquisition of territory that was previously unin-
habited or is not recognized as belonging to another political entity.

As can be seen from this typology, two fundamental kinds of
acquisition are recognized. The first type, which includes conquest,
cession and annexation, presumes the land to be inhabited. Hence,
legislation will always be drafted with the rights of the inhabitants
firmly in mind. In the second type (settlement), given that there are no
original inhabitants, the law will develop without attending to these
concerns. Thus, taking a piece of property as an example, in the former
case, the property will be obtained in some manner from the previous
owner, whereas in the latter case the property can be granted directly
to new colonists without concern for the former owners.

If the test of "occupancy," as it developed in the colonial era, had
been truly objective by modern standards, such division between the
two types of acquisition would be highly rational. However, if the
definition were based on ethnocentric biases, mistakes could easily be
made. As it happens, in colonial history, the latter occurred. Occupation, for example, in the mid-eighteenth century—at the height of
British colonial expansion—was equated with cultivation, so that
unoccupied land became, in the legal view, not based on the criterion of
presence or absence of people, but rather on whether or not the people
used the land for agriculture. This view is illustrated most forcefully
by Lord Blackstone, a leading English scholar of his time, who in his
authoritative commentary on the laws of England, written in 1765,
defined the typological opposition between "occupied" and "unoccupied" acquisition as follows (Tucker 1803: 107-08):

> Plantations or colonies, in distinct countries, are either such
> where the lands are claimed by right of occupancy only, by
> finding them desert and uncultivated, and peopling them
> from the mother country; or where, when already cultivated,
> they have been either gained, by conquest, or ceded to us by
> treaties. And both these rights are founded upon the law of
> nature, or at least upon that of nations. But there is a differ-
> ence between these two species of colonies, with respect to
> the laws by which they are bound. For it hath been held, that
> if an uninhabited country be discovered and planted by
> English subjects, all the English laws then in being, which are
> the birthright of every subject, are immediately there in
> force. . . . But conquered or ceded countries, that have already
> laws of their own, the king may indeed alter and change those
> laws; but, till he does actually change them, the ancient laws
> of the country remain. . . .

Given the existence of such ethnocentric biases, it is not hard to imagine that there were situations in which the colonists passed the kind of laws appropriate for unoccupied territories on lands that, as can be shown by contemporary standards, were occupied. In such cases, something unique took place. The ruler at the time, not perceiving that in future these lands would be considered occupied, passed legislation that was silent with regard to the rights of the (now presumed to be) original owners.

Under such circumstances, it is fair to ask whether English legal tradition recognizes that the descendants of the aboriginal peoples still own their lands. It is a question replete with ambiguity. On the one hand, legislation enacted in such circumstances would appear to have had the result of extinguishing these rights; on the other, in contrast to the principles of English law, the ruler would not have enunciated a clear policy to do so. The issue to resolve, then, is whether the legislation passed did extinguish these rights, notwithstanding the fact that it is silent on the subject. If it did, then one point is certain. Under English law the possibility that the legislative tradition may have erred in assuming that the territory was unoccupied is irrelevant: the rights of the aboriginal peoples no longer exist.

This point can be exemplified by reference to a decision made in an Australian case (Milirrupum 1970). Australian legal tradition is based on the assumption that, prior to contact, all lands were unoccupied. The Aborigines who brought up the case provided evidence that this presumption was in error, that they did have a system of land tenure, which the colonists should have recognized. In making a decision, Mr. Justice Blackburn, while appearing to accept the factual accuracy of this assertion, nonetheless ruled against the Aborigines. His reasoning relied, among other matters, on the conclusion that Australian legislation, despite the fact that it was based on an erroneous assumption, still had the effect of cancelling Aboriginal property rights. He stated (*ibid.*: 243-44):

> For present purposes, the decision is an authority binding on this Court that New South Wales was a settled or peaceably occupied colony. Mr. Woodward [counsel for the aboriginal plaintiffs] contended that the statement of their Lordships that New South Wales was "a colony which consisted of a tract of territory practically unoccupied, without settled inhabitants or settled law" was a statement which was historically inaccurate, particularly in the light of modern anthropological knowledge; the very evidence in this case, Mr. Woodward contended, was that the subject land, at any rate, was not without settled inhabitants or settled law; indeed, he said, the evidence showed that the subject land had

highly settled inhabitants and settled law. In my opinion, in the light of the authorities . . . the question is one not of fact but of law. Whether or not the Australian aboriginals living in any part of New South Wales had in 1728 a system of law which was beyond the powers of the settlers at that time to perceive or comprehend, it is beyond the power of this court to decide otherwise than that New South Wales came into the category of a settled or occupied colony.

In short, the Australian court refused to recognize the continued existence of aboriginal rights—despite new facts—in the face of a body of tradition and legislation based on the erroneous assumption that the land was unoccupied at the time of contact. This unfortunate ruling was undone only through the enactment of new legislation that explicitly recognized the existence of aboriginal rights in Australian law.[2]

In sum, the descendants of aboriginal peoples presently living in nation-states bound to English legal tradition must overcome two obstacles to establish their aboriginal rights in courts. First, they must convince the court to accept the fact that the rights asserted are reconcilable with British legal tradition. Second, they must gain court acceptance of the fact that these rights remain in place despite general legislation passed by state authorities. Failure of the first task means that in the view of the courts the aboriginal peoples in question never had any rights. Failure of the second means that although the courts may agree that aboriginal peoples did once have such rights, they were extinguished by general legislation and no longer exist.

THE CANADIAN SITUATION

The aboriginal peoples of Canada are no exception to this conclusion. However, their circumstances do have one advantage over the Australian case cited above. It relates to the question of legal traditions. Although it is true that, following Lester (1981: 161f), Canadian law has developed on the assumption that Canadian territory was not previously occupied, one can point to innumerable exceptions to this proposition. Most obvious are the numbered treaties, such as those in the Prairies, in which the Crown actively sought and obtained land cessions in return for specific compensation and rights, before opening up a region for settlement. There are also instances in which the sovereign recognized and affirmed the rights of aboriginal peoples, as in the Royal Proclamation of 1763 and in the act that transferred the territory of Rupert's Land to Canada. This can be seen, as well, in the concern expressed by federal authorities when lands, such as those in British Columbia, were opened up for occupancy by colonists before obtaining cessions from the original inhabitants. In short, given our legal history, it would not be as easy for the courts in this country to dismiss the claims of aboriginal peoples by recourse to an unambiguous (if erroneous) legal belief that, at contact, the land was completely unoccupied.

Although the Canadian court system had heard many cases concerning the interpretation of aboriginal peoples' rights in instances (such as the Royal Proclamation of 1763 and the treaties) where the sovereign had spoken (through legislation or treaties), it was not until 1969 that it was called upon to decide a case in which *de facto* expropriation of rights had occurred, and in which the sovereign had not spoken. Known as the "Nishga case" (after the aboriginal nation by that name) or the "Calder case" (after the Nishga chief who brought forward the case), through it Canadian aboriginal peoples first came to know whether the Canadian court system accepted or rejected the idea that they possessed aboriginal rights at the time of first contact, and whether these rights had managed to survive the general legislation that the state subsequently enacted.

The actual question asked of the courts was framed in a manner to elicit the widest possible positive interpretation with the least overall risk to the interests of the Nishga. Specifically, it limited the aboriginal right in question to "an interest which is usufructuary in nature; a tribal interest inalienable except to the Crown and extinguishable only by legislative enactment" (Calder 1973: 173). As such, it focussed the discussion on the one aspect of aboriginal rights that the sovereign in Canada appeared (in other pronouncements such as treaties and the Royal Proclamation of 1763) to have been most careful in acknowledging: the right to use collectively and occupy the land for the purposes of hunting, fishing and trapping. As well, the suit limited the temporal component to the determination of whether the legislative acts of the colony of British Columbia and the crown colony of Vancouver Island had extinguished these rights in the period prior to Confederation.

In order to establish this right, Nishga lawyers Mr. (later Justice) Berger and Mr. Rosenbloom brought forward evidence on three points. The first was to establish, through the direct testimony of Nishga witnesses and of Wilson Duff, an anthropologist with long working experience among Northwest Coast groups, that at the time of contact the Nishga had a system of land tenure that was "reconcilable with Canadian law." Second, they introduced documents that purported to extend the intent of the sovereign to respect usufructuary rights to all Indians of British Columbia. Specifically, they argued that by force of the Royal Proclamation of 1763 (*ibid.*: 127) Indians "should not be molested or disturbed in the Possession of such parts of our Dominions and Territories as, not having been ceded to or purchased by us, are reserved to them or any of them, as Hunting Grounds." And that this right was extended to the Northwest Coast Indians by virtue of the statement:

> And we do further declare it to be Our Royal Will and Pleasure, . . . to reserve under our Sovereignty, Protection and Dominion, for the use of the said Indians, all the Lands and Territories not included within the Limits of Our said Three new Governments, or within the Limits of the Territory granted to the Hudson's Bay Company, as also all the Lands and Territories lying to the westward of the sources of the Rivers which fall into the Sea from the West and North West. . . .

Third, the lawyers introduced documents and expert testimony of a historian to show that the colonial legislature during the period in question had not passed any acts expressly extinguishing aboriginal title. And since the Government of Canada had not done so in the period since Confederation, they argued that the Nishga still possessed the aboriginal right to use and occupy these lands.

For their part, the lawyers representing the government of British Columbia, the defendant in this case, argued that whatever claim based on aboriginal title (and they questioned whether such title had existed in the pre-contact period) the Nishga may have had, it had been extinguished, albeit without having been expressly mentioned, by the general intent of the legislation passed by the colonial authorities in the pre-Confederation period. As their evidence, they included a series of land-use and other legislative acts passed by the relevant colonial authorities in that period.

The case was tried in April 1969, and in October, Justice Gould handed down his decision. The judge agreed with the provincial government's position and argued that if any aboriginal title existed, it had been extinguished by the legislation of the colonial period. He thus dismissed the claim. However, in his judgement he did not express a view on whether the Nishga had had an aboriginal title to be extinguished. In 1970, the case was taken to the British Columbia Court of Appeal. In May of that year, a decision again unfavourable to the Nishga claim, was expressed unanimously by Justices Davey, Tysoe and Maclean. Their reason was identical to that of Justice Gould.

However, unlike the trial judge, the Court of Appeal did express an opinion as to whether the Nishga possessed the kind of law that was congruent with Canadian law. Chief Justice Davey said they did not. He argued (Calder 1970: 483):

> . . . in spite of the commendation of Mr. Duff, a well-known anthropologist, of the native culture of the Indians on the

mainland of British Columbia, they were undoubtedly at the time of settlement a very primitive people with few of the institutions of civilized society, and none at all of our notions of private property. . . .

Therefore, he went on:

> I see no evidence to justify a conclusion that the aboriginal rights claimed by the successors of these primitive people are of a kind that it should be assumed the Crown recognized them when it acquired the mainland of British Columbia by occupation.

This, he compared to the situation in some parts of Africa,

> . . . in which the territory of a people was ceded to the British Crown following conquest. The inhabitants had definite notions of rights of private property in specific pieces of land although of a communal, tribal and family nature, which it was presumed the Crown intended to respect and recognize and intended to be supported by the municipal courts.

Thus, the Court of Appeal rejected the Nishga claim not only because legislation had extinguished their rights but because, in their view, Nishga society was too primitive to possess laws that a new sovereign would be able to recognize.

In November 1971, the case was appealed to the Supreme Court of Canada. It was heard by a court consisting of seven justices that included, in order of seniority, Martland, Judson, Ritchie, Hall, Spence, Pigeon and Laskin. The court reserved judgement for over a year, finally rendering its opinion on the last day of January of 1973.

Of the seven justices, six dealt with the substantive issue of aboriginal rights. One, Justice Pigeon, dealt only with the technical question of whether an action of this nature could be brought against the Province of British Columbia in the absence of legislation allowing suits against the Crown. He concluded that it could not, and so decided against the Nishga.

The remaining six justices dealt in some detail with all of the substantive points raised in the Nishga suit. Their determination on these issues was conveyed in two opinions: one written by Justice Judson with the concurrence of Justices Martland and Ritchie, the other by Justice Hall, supported by Justices Spence and Laskin.

Regarding the first test of aboriginal rights, both opinions agreed. The Nishga, despite the opinion of the Court of Appeal, did possess, at the time of contact, rights that were reconcilable with English law. According to Justice Judson (Calder 1973: 156): "the fact is that when the settlers came, the Indians were there, organized in societies and occupying the land as their forefathers had done for centuries. This is what Indian title means. . . ." In his opinion, Justice Hall made it clear that the Court of Appeal had erred in interpretation when taking its position (*ibid.*: 169-70):

> The assessment and interpretation of historical documents and enactments tendered in evidence must be approached in the light of present-day research and knowledge, disregarding ancient concepts formulated when understanding of the customs and cultures of our original people was rudimentary and incomplete and when they were thought to be wholly without cohesion, laws, or culture, in effect a subhuman species. . . .

After citing the opinion of Chief Justice Davey of the Court of Appeal, he concluded, "In so saying this in 1970, he [Chief Justice Davey] was assessing the Indian culture of 1858 by the same standards that Europeans applied to the Indians of North America two or more centuries before." However, when the evidence is examined in the light of contemporary knowledge, he continued, there is no problem in finding that whether the land was acquired by "discovery or conquest" (*ibid.*: 208) the Nishga had a code of law reconcilable with British tradition.

The court also agreed, although using different logic, that British recognition of this title during the colonial period should be acknowledged. Three judges, Hall, Spence and Laskin, argued that such recognition derives directly from the application of the Royal Proclamation of 1763 to British Columbia, for, according to Hall, the authors of this proclamation were well aware of the existence of such an area and intended to include it when they stated that the proclamation extended to all "Lands and Territories lying to the westward of the source of the Rivers which fall into the Sea from the North and Northwest . . ." The other three justices, following Justice Judson's opinion, argued that the Royal Proclamation did not apply to the region. However, they argued "Indian title" need not depend upon the conscious recognition by the sovereign, but rather derives from the fact that the Indians had been there for centuries, organized into societies.

It was over the second fundamental question that opinions were divided evenly: whether such title continued to exist in the face of colonial legislation. Justices Judson, Martland and Ritchie argued that it did not, for in their view the legislative acts of the colonial period were intended to be general legislation and therefore had the effect of extinguishing aboriginal title to lands. They decided against the Nishga suit.

The three remaining justices took the opposite position on this point. They argued that, once recognized, aboriginal title, like the title of any people under English law, could not be extinguished without specific legislation. To this end, Justice Hall cited two significant precedents. The first referred to an opinion by Lord Denning of the House of Lords when he spoke in 1975 as the highest appeal authority in Commonwealth Law (quoted in Calder 1973: 209): "in inquiring, however, what rights are recognized, there is one guiding principle. It is this: The courts will assume that (in acquired territories) the British Crown intends that the rights of property of the inhabitants are to be fully respected." The second precedent referred to an opinion by American Justice Davis, who in a 1967 case respecting the Lipan Apache Tribe, stated (quoted in Calder 1973: 210): "In the absence of a 'clear and plain indication' in the public records that the sovereign 'intended to extinguish all of the [claimants'] rights in their property, Indian title continues. . . ." Thus, Justice Hall concluded (*ibid.*): "It would, accordingly, appear to be beyond question that the onus of proving that the Sovereign intended to extinguish the Indian title lies on the respondent [the Province of British Columbia] and that intention must be 'clear and plain.' There is no such proof in the case at bar; no legislation to that effect." In fact, he suggested that the documentary evidence for the period indicates to the contrary that the colonial authorities were not given any "power or authorization to extinguish Indian title" (*ibid.*: 217). As a result, he supported the Nishga claim that their aboriginal title still remains in effect and could be enforced through court action.

Although the Nishga lost their case on a 4 to 3 judgement, the decision represented something of a new departure. It established, first of all, the certainty that at least one aboriginal group possessed rights at the time of contact that were reconcilable with Canadian law. Second, and more significantly, there was the strong possibility that at least one of these rights—the usufruct title, in at least the Nass Valley of British Columbia—had survived colonial legislation and was still in existence. Hence, the case asserted the possibility that aboriginal peoples, unlike Australian Aborigines, still possessed rights that the contemporary court would recognize as existing, and therefore uphold.[3]

In the period since the Calder decision, judicial opinion has tended to support this proposition. Perhaps in the light of the strong majority in the Supreme Court, other judges have shown a willingness to extend the notion of reconcilable law to other groups, such as the Baker Lake Inuit and the James Bay Cree. Given the wide cultural diversity between the Nishga, the Cree and the Inuit, it seems fair to conclude that this proposition has gained acceptability in the courts. Judicial opinion, in the same cases cited above, supported the idea that aboriginal property rights cannot be extinguished except by specific legislation and hence that certain rights may have survived and are enforceable today.

However, although the courts, since the Calder decision, recognize the survival of some aboriginal rights, they have consistently taken the position that these rights can be modified, limited and abridged by laws that do not explicitly mention aboriginal rights. In the Nishga case, for example, although the Supreme Court held that the Indians of British Columbia have a right to hunt and fish on unoccupied land protected by the Royal Proclamation of 1763, in 1976 they ruled that native fishermen, nonetheless, were subject to the same regulations as non-native fishermen under existing federal legislation, even though the legislation did not speak to the point (Derriksan 1976). In the following year, the court went further and unanimously agreed that Indians in British Columbia, even if protected by the Royal Proclamation of 1763, must conform to the same hunting regulations as non-native hunters, unless it could be expressly demonstrated that to do so would inhibit their "status and capacity" as Indians (Kruger 1977). In short, the courts have, on the one hand, accepted the existence of an aboriginal right, while, on the other, they have restricted it so that it has no more substance than the privileges extended to any resident. In the Baker Lake case, Justice Mahoney extended this general line of reasoning specifically to aboriginal title. Citing specific Supreme Court decisions, he declared (Baker Lake 1980: 244): "If aboriginal title that arose in Rupert's Land (now the Northwest Territories) . . . were a proprietary right then it would necessarily have been extinguished by the Royal Charter of May 2, 1670 which granted the Hudson's Bay Company ownership of the entire colony."

There have been no court actions in which aboriginal rights in the sense of political rights has been at issue. Nor has there been any indication as to how the courts might view an assertion such as an unextinguished right to self-government, in light of the Calder decision. However, an examination of precedents indicates that it would be highly unlikely that such a proposition would be upheld. For, although the courts would probably be willing to accept that pre-contact aboriginal peoples had a form of self-government and might even accept factual evidence showing its continuity into the present, they would deny that political rights survived legislation that established, for example, the parliamentary form of government for all citizens, including aboriginal peoples. The courts could also take a second line of reasoning and declare that because claims to self-government concern sovereignty, they lie outside the judicial competence of the domestic courts of this country. Such a declaration might imply, in principle, that the case should be taken into the international judicial arena. However, given that such tribunals as the International Court of Justice are empowered only to hear cases in which sovereignty already has international recognition, no native groups would have the standing necessary to bring forth the action. Hence, one can conclude that there is no judicial forum in which aboriginal rights as political rights could be established.

CONCLUSIONS: ABORIGINAL RIGHTS AND THE LAW

As we have seen in this chapter, in order to make a case for their rights, an aboriginal people must demonstrate that their law at the time of contact was recognizable in British eyes, and that their rights remain unextinguished in the present. In Canada, our legal traditions have developed primarily around the proposition that, in principle, the aboriginal peoples were too primitive to have such rights. As a result, our legal traditions developed in such a way that the possible consequences of legislation on the status of native rights were virtually ignored. It was presumed that unless the sovereign had spoken, no aboriginal group retained its rights into the present.

This legal tradition remained in place until the Supreme Court decision was made in the Calder case in 1973. This decision established the principle that aboriginal societies did exist at the time of contact in a form that demanded the recognition of their rights in the courts, regardless of the fact that they were not recognized at the time. It also established the strong possibility that at least some of their rights remained in existence up to the present day. As such, the Nishga decision forced a recasting of Canadian legal traditions into a framework that conforms with a view called "cultural relativity," which states that no culture can be properly seen as inferior to another. When cast in this light, Nishga society became transformed from primitive to an equal. Hence, like any other people who are under English law, its members retained the right to have their property and title to land respected and protected by the new sovereign (until expressly extinguished by legislation and compensation paid) and thus had the standing to seek legal protection should it be necessary.

This landmark decision is not without its drawbacks. Although the principle has been established, it still remains necessary to prove a society is 'civilized' to obtain standing in court. The problem with this situation is illustrated in the Baker Lake case. According to Justice Mahoney (Baker Lake 1980: 227): "The fact is that the aboriginal Inuit had an organized society. It was not a society with very elaborate institutions but it was a society organized to exploit the resources available on the barrens and essential to sustain human life there. That was about all they could do: hunt and fish and survive." Such a view runs counter to the principle of cultural relativity, and appears, in a veiled form, as an attempt to return to earlier notions based on an evolutionary bias. Clearly, ethnocentric biases die hard. Another problem is that the courts appear unwilling to undo, by themselves, the practical implications of this change in principle. An example of this is found in their use of notions such as "abridgement" to blunt the actual effect of an unextinguished aboriginal right.

Such examples as these have led some observers to believe that the Canadian courts may be unwilling to provide a detailed judicial definition of the substance of aboriginal rights. It is a prediction that may well prove correct over time. Yet, even if this were to be the case, the significance of recent court decisions, and in particular of the Calder judgement, would not be diminished. The Calder case firmly established a legal concept of singular importance: that even within the ideological orientation of English legal tradition, aboriginal peoples could be shown to have rights that originated prior to contact and that could exist without express acknowledgement by a British or Canadian sovereign. In other words, it defined for Canadian law the fundamental principle of aboriginal rights.

NOTES

1. A version of this chapter was published in French under the title "Regard Anthropologique sur la Définition Judicaire des Droits Autochotones" (Asch 1983b).
2. For a fuller discussion of the Australian case, see Maddock (1980).
3. For a discussion of the legal implications of the Calder decision, see Lysyk (1973) and Sanders (1978).

5

THE EVOLUTION OF FEDERAL POLICY ON ABORIGINAL RIGHTS

The topic for this chapter should have been a description of the current positions of the federal and provincial governments on the constitutional meaning of aboriginal rights. This cannot be done—not because the governments have no *position* on the subject, but because they have not stated them in any great detail. It therefore becomes necessary to construct their views indirectly, on the basis of *policies* developed in their transactions with native peoples. Although some provinces (Quebec and Alberta) have aboriginal policies, it is only the federal government that has developed a detailed policy. For the sake of clarity, therefore, I shall restrict this discussion to federal policy.

The current federal position was first articulated at the March 1983 First Ministers' Conference. In part, it stated (*Globe and Mail*, 16 March 1983):

> the rights of the aboriginal peoples to the use and occupancy of land and their rights to fish, hunt, trap and gather, based on traditional and continuing use and occupancy as recognized by treaties and land claims settlements,

> the preservation and enhancement of the use by the aboriginal peoples of their own cultures, customs, traditions, religions and languages, including the education of their children within their own languages, as well as within one of the official languages of Canada, in order that their children may be equipped to live in the cultural milieu of their choice,

> the institution of various forms of aboriginal governments within the Constitution of Canada and under the laws of Canada to meet the respective needs of their communities and aggregations of communities.

Although brief and rather general, the statement is most useful for it provides two important insights into the federal position on aboriginal rights. The first relates to content; namely, that contemporary aboriginal societies are acknowledged to be autonomous cultures that have the right to an ongoing existence within Canada, and that one specific attribute of that existence is the constitutional recognition of some kind of self-government. In other words, the statement strongly implies that in the current view of the federal government, aboriginal rights may include political as well as property rights. It is, as I shall elaborate below, a change in stance of some importance.

The second insight is that their policy orientation on aboriginal rights in general, as it is reflected in this statement and interventions at the conference, is consistent with other recent expressions of policy objectives concerning native peoples and their lands. This means that, in principle, it would be possible to deduce some of the detail concerning their notion of aboriginal rights through an examination of policy in these other related areas. Unfortunately, for most aspects of policy, the federal position has advanced little from the general kind of rhetoric contained in the conference statement cited here. However, there is one important exception. It concerns policy on aboriginal lands that remained unceded to the Crown at the time of the Calder decision in 1973. In this policy area, called "Comprehensive Claims Policy," the federal government has developed a framework that it perceives would guarantee the kinds of aboriginal rights contained in the conference statement cited above. An examination of the general pronouncements and the results of particular land-claims negotiations covered under the terms of this policy therefore provides a source for understanding the government's interpretation of the constitutional meaning of aboriginal rights.

The primary focus of this chapter, then, is on the current federal position concerning the meaning of aboriginal rights. I shall also discuss the evolution of the current stance with the intention of showing the degree to which current policy represents a clear break from earlier positions. As well, I shall describe the factual basis upon which one could have concluded, even without the explicit acknowledgement contained in Calder, that British and Canadian governments did formulate their policies and practices on the assumption that aboriginal peoples possessed certain rights (including perhaps political rights) independently of their recognition by the state. It is a notion that finds its clearest expression in the method used historically to acquire the lands of the aboriginal peoples.

LAND ACQUISITION POLICY PRIOR TO THE CALDER CASE

Traditional state policy respecting the acquisition of aboriginal lands can be used to deduce an acknowledgement of aboriginal rights in two ways. The first pertains to the presumed existence of such rights in the minds of the colonists. If these lands were not acquired through some form of transaction, be it purchase or even conquest, then it could be argued that the colonists had no notion of aboriginal peoples' owning any property at all. Thus, whenever colonists obtained lands through purchase they would be acknowledging that, at least at the time of the transaction, the aboriginal peoples possessed some interest that could be acquired. Hence, although the nature of the interest may have remained unspecified, the fact of the transaction itself indicates that it must have existed prior to purchase. In this sense, then, the acquisition of lands from native peoples could be viewed as the purchase of an aboriginal interest.

The second relates to the possible content of this aboriginal interest as perceived by the government when it purchased such lands. In order to purchase land, the state, typically, entered into written agreements with aboriginal holders. Although the terms of the written versions of these agreements are often challenged by the descendants of the aboriginal holders, the state appears content to acknowledge their legitimacy. These clauses, especially in the post-Confederation period, often specify obligations and benefits beyond those anticipated in a property transaction to include factors of a social or political contractual nature. An examination of these terms can provide an insight into the government's perception of the content of the rights and help to form an impression of the government's view of the nature and viability of the group that possessed them.

STATE ACKNOWLEDGEMENT OF A NATIVE INTEREST

As the evidence from early land-purchase agreements attest, there can be no doubt but that private colonists accepted, from the very onset of colonization, that aboriginal peoples possessed tangible interests related to land that could be acquired through purchase. Indeed, the notion was so commonly held that one of the most endemic problems that arose in the seventeenth and eighteenth centuries, in particular, was the willingness on the part of colonists to enter into contracts, often of a highly suspicious nature, with aboriginal peoples.[1]

The state did intervene in land transactions in part to quell the discontent expressed by native groups because of these sharp practices. However, it was not until 1763 that the British authorities introduced their first general policy (in the Royal Proclamation) on the state's role in land acquisition. This policy stipulates that (1) no one except the representative of the sovereign is authorized to purchase aboriginal lands; (2) the formalization of the transfer must be made by an authorized representative of the aboriginal group; (3) the transfer must take place at a public meeting attended by the other members of the aboriginal group (this is, of course, the origin of the formula used to legitimize later land transactions and in particular the treaties signed in the period following Confederation); and (4) most importantly, the policy (for full text, see Appendix B) also asserts (Royal Proclamation 1763) that:

> . . . whereas it is just and reasonable, and essential to our
> interest, and the security of our Colonies, that the several
> Nations or Tribes of Indians with whom we are connected,
> and who live under our protection, should not be molested or
> disturbed in the Possession of such Parts of our Dominions
> and Territories as, not having been ceded to or purchased by
> Us, are reserved to them or any of them as their Hunting
> Grounds.

Whereas the location of these lands and the content of the interest
implied by the phrase "reserved as their Hunting Grounds" is open to
interpretation,[2] it is clear that the document does acknowledge that
such lands exist and that the aboriginal peoples who occupy and use
them have an interest that is obtainable through cession or purchase.
Although the Royal Proclamation does not say so directly, it could be
inferred that the "Hunting Grounds" could well include aboriginal
lands that had been held prior to first contact.

In 1867, the Canadian authorities acquired legislative independence
through the British North America Act. In 1869, they introduced a
policy respecting the acquisition of lands held by native peoples in
territory transferred to Canada through the purchase of the Hudson's
Bay Company's interests in Rupert's Land. The core of this policy is
contained in an Order-in-Council addressed to the British sovereign
by Parliament in 1870: ". . . upon the transference of the territories in
question to the Canadian government, the claims of the Indian tribes
to compensation for land required for the purposes of settlement will
be considered and settled in conformity with the equitable principles
which have uniformly governed the British Crown in its dealings with
the aboriginals" (Statutes Order 1870:264). It is a statement that
confirms, albeit in different terms, the view of a tangible pre-existing
aboriginal interest, implied by the Royal Proclamation of 1763.

Yet, the statement does not have a blanket policy on the acquisition
of aboriginal lands. Rather, it focusses only on those cases where the
territory is "required for settlement." In practice, this meant that the
policy was applied only after large-scale colonial settlement appeared
imminent. Thus, in Rupert's Land—from Treaty 1, signed in 1871,
covering the eastern region of Manitoba to Treaty 11, signed in1921,
covering the Mackenzie Valley region in the Northwest Territories,
there is a movement in the dates and locales of these transactions that
coincides with the westward and northward patterns of migration and
settlement. As a result, after the last treaty was signed in 1923, there
were still large tracts of aboriginal lands in British Columbia, the
Yukon, the Northwest Territories, Quebec and the Atlantic provinces
for which cession agreements had not been reached. The question,

then, facing the government was whether claims of ownership that originated with these groups would be honoured.

In the period between 1923 and 1969, the government took no position on the issue. However, in the 1969 White Paper on Indian Policy (DIAND 1969: 11), the government came to the conclusion that "other (grievances) relate to aboriginal claims to land. These are so general and undefined that it is not realistic to think of them as specific claims capable of remedy except through a policy and program that will end injustice to Indians as members of the Canadian community." In other words, government decided not to honour the claims. Yet, it is important to note that, even in this harshest of pronouncements, the government's rejection is due to the vagueness of the claims, which renders them "incapable of remedy," rather than to a denial in principle that the tangible good upon which the claim is based exists.

THE GOVERNMENT'S VIEW OF THE CONTENT OF THE NATIVE INTEREST
As the foregoing discussion indicates, the recognition of an aboriginal interest exists from the first moments of colonial history. The terms of early land-transfer agreements confirm that at least one aspect of this pre-existing interest, as viewed by colonists, pertains to the lands aboriginal peoples use and occupy. As well, the content of the agreements reveals that this interest can be held by aboriginal peoples collectively, and is obtainable in exchange for tangible goods. However, since these agreements generally do not mention factors other than those pertaining directly to property, it is difficult to use them to extract the colonists' perceptions of the non-property features of the aboriginal interest.

In contrast, the written versions of post-Confederation treaties, and especially the eleven numbered treaties, contain a wide range of propositions that are both of a property and social-contractual nature. Furthermore, although they were completed with very different cultural groups in widely disparate regions over a span of more than fifty years, their terms remain remarkably consistent in content. An examination of these treaties, then, should provide the kind of information upon which to formulate the image held by government of the aboriginal interest for at least half a century. Indeed, this view remained constant throughout a period of 130 years, from about 1830 to 1969.

Typical of the obligations and benefits contained in all the numbered treaties are those found in Treaty 4. It was signed in 1874 at Qu'Appelle and Fort Ellice in what is now the province of Saskatchewan between the representatives of the Queen and a number of Cree and Saulteaux bands. (For full text, see Appendix C.)

According to the government version, Treaty 4 has two primary purposes. The first is "to obtain the consent" of the "Indian subjects . . . to open up for settlement, immigration, trade and . . . other purposes," the tract of land these aboriginal peoples are said to inhabit. The second is to insure "that there will be peace and good will" between the Indians and the Crown and "between them and Her Majesty's other subjects."

The stated property-related obligation of the aboriginal people is to "cede, release, surrender and yield up . . . all the rights, titles and privileges" to the lands specified in the agreement. Including most of south-central Saskatchewan, the area is said, in the letter of transmittal, to encompass about 50,000 square miles. The beneficiary of this transfer is stated to be "the Government of the Dominion of Canada, Her Majesty the Queen, and Her successors forever. . . ."

In addition to a requirement to transfer lands, Treaty 4 also specifies a number of social-contractual obligations to be undertaken by the aboriginal peoples incorporated within the treaty. These include the agreement to:

> . . . strictly observe this Treaty; conduct and behave them-
> selves as good and loyal subjects of Her Majesty the Queen; in
> all respects to obey and abide by the law; maintain peace and
> good order between each other and between themselves and
> other tribes of Indians; maintain peace and good order
> between themselves and others of Her Majesty's subjects,
> whether Indians, Half Breeds, or whites not inhabiting or
> hereafter to inhabit any part of the . . . ceded tract; not molest
> the person or property of any inhabitant of the ceded tract or
> the property of Her Majesty the Queen; not interfere with or
> trouble any person passing or travelling through the said
> tract, or any part thereof; assist the officers of Her Majesty in
> bringing to justice and punishment any Indian attending
> against the stipulations of this treaty, or infringing the laws
> in force in the country so ceded.

According to the language of the treaty, these obligations are undertaken by the "undersigned Chiefs and Head men on their own behalf and on behalf of all other Indians inhabiting the tract within ceded." In return for signing the agreement, the government undertakes to provide certain benefits to the people. These are to include land, education, financial benefits, hunting and trapping benefits and benefits to encourage the development of agriculture.

With respect to land, the government promises that it will protect a portion of the lands ceded. The amount of those protected lands or reserves will be determined after a census is taken, on the basis of a formula of one square mile for each family of five. With respect to education, the government, on a continuing basis, will "maintain a school in the reserve allotted to each band as soon as they settle on said reserve and are prepared for a teacher." The financial provisions include a one-time gift of $25 to each chief, $15 to each headman (not to exceed four in each band) and $12 for every other Indian person in the band and annual payments of similar, though not quite identical, amounts to all head members.

Hunting and trapping benefits include an annual payment in kind of $750 worth of powder, shot, ball and twine, to be distributed among all the lands of the region. As well, the Queen promises on behalf of the Canadian government, that:

> Her said Indians shall have right to pursue their avocations of hunting, trapping and fishing throughout the tract sur- rendered, subject to such regulations as may from time to time be made by the Government of the country . . . and saving and excepting such tracts as may be required for settlement, mining or other purposes, under grant or other rights given by Her Majesty's government.

Finally, the treaty obliges the government to undertake the follow- ing with respect to the development of agriculture:

> . . . the following articles shall be supplied to any band . . . who are now actually cultivating the soil, or who shall hereafter settle on their reserves and commence to break up the land, that is to say: two hoes, one spade, one scythe, and one axe for every family so actually cultivating, and enough seed, wheat, barley, oats and potatoes to plant such land as they have taken up; also one plough and two burrows for every ten families so cultivating . . ., and also to each Chief for the use of his band . . . one yoke of oxen, one bull, four cows, a chest of ordinary carpenter's tools, five handsaws, five augers, one crosscut saw, one pit-saw, the necessary files and one grind- stone, all the aforesaid articles to be given, and for all, for the encouragement of the practice of agriculture among the Indians.

The provisions respecting property and the protection of hunting are self-evident. However, the undertakings concerning education, sedentarization and agriculture require additional explanation. In part, they are included because government perceived that aboriginal society would become transformed by the influx of settlers who were to arrive. In part, they also reflected an ideological premise dominant at the time. This belief was founded on the assumption that aboriginal peoples were less advanced, not because of an inherent biological inferiority, but rather because of the inferiority of their "way of life." Therefore, once their "primitive" institutions and values had been replaced by "civilized" ones, their potential for equality would be realized (Upton 1973). That is, as Morris (1973: 39) suggests, beginning in the 1830s, the object of British rule was "to tackle the evils of slavery, ignorance and paganism at source, to teach the simpler people the benefits of steam, free trade and revealed religion, and to establish not a world empire in the Napoleonic sense but a moral empire of loftier interest." Thus, to some degree the provisions were based on the assumption that, once aboriginal peoples encountered the benefits of 'civilization,' they would self-destruct, and its members would become assimilated into the Canadian mainstream.[3] It is an orientation to aboriginal policy that was applied in the Canadian colonies as early as the 1830s (Upton 1973) and became adopted by the Canadian authorities after Confederation in 1867.

Seen in this light, the benefits pertaining to agriculture, reserve lands and education found in the numbered treaties can be understood as an expression of the government's desire to ease the inevitable transition that would take place in aboriginal society. Thus, one must presume that the benefits were regarded as temporary measures of a humanitarian nature.

The policy of gradualism contained in the treaty provisions was met with criticism by those in government who advocated a more rapid assimilationist approach. However, gradualism prevailed in official policy until the late 1960s. Thus, as late as 1920, one year before the last of the numbered treaties was signed, Duncan Campbell Scott, superintendent-general of the Indian Affairs Branch could state in public testimony, concerning a proposed bill on Indian policy (DIAND 1975: 122-23):

> I want to get rid of the Indian problem. I do not think as a matter of fact, that the country ought to continuously protect a class of people who are able to stand alone. That is my whole point. I do not want to pass into the citizens class people who are paupers. That is not the intension of the Bill. But after one hundred years, after being in close contact with civilization it is unnerving to the individual or to a band to continue the state of tutelege, when he or they are able to take this position as British Citizen or Canadian Citizenship to support themselves and stand alone. That has been the whole purpose of education and advancement since earlier times.
>
> Our object is to continue until there is not a single Indian in

Canada that has not been absorbed into the body politic and there is no Indian question and no Indian problem.

With the election of Prime Minister Trudeau in 1968, the advocates of a rapid assimilationist orientation finally had a supporter at the highest level of government. The new direction was announced in the White Paper on Indian Policy in 1969 (DIAND 1969: 1). It was based on the belief that the gradualist approach had worked to reinforce "segregation" and "discrimination" and hence to act as an impediment to assimilation: "The policies proposed recognize the simple reality that the separate legal status of Indians and the policies which have flowed from it have kept the Indian people apart from and behind other Canadians."

Accordingly, the government proposed to terminate all relationships with Indians that fostered the gradualist approach, and to replace them with policies to encourage rapid integration of the aboriginal population into the dominant society. With respect to treaty benefits, Prime Minister Trudeau stated (Cumming and Mickenberg 1972: 331):

It's inconceivable, I think, that in a society one section of the society have a treaty with the other section of the society. We must be all equal under the laws and we must not sign treaties amongst ourselves . . . I don't think that we should encourage Indians to feel these treaties should last forever within Canada. . . They should become Canadians as all other Canadians.

He thus revealed the continued belief in the temporary nature of these provisions.

During this period the Metis peoples were not considered to be aboriginal peoples. Government policy, therefore, did not acknowledge any need for even such temporary measures as treaties to ease their transition to assimilation. In principle, government believed Metis were assimilated. Although this perception may appear to reflect a negative assessment of their cultural distinctiveness, it need not be interpreted in this manner. With assimilation came the right to participate in the institutions of 'civilization' and, in particular, in government. With their majority standing at the time of the making of the province of Manitoba in 1871, the Metis seemed to have found a solution to the maintenance of their political rights as aboriginal peoples on a permanent rather than a transitional basis. However, the temporary nature of this solution soon became apparent when, in the period from 1871 to 1885, the population of Manitoba increased from

12,000 (of which the overwhelming majority were Metis or French-speaking) to over 110,000 (of which only a small minority were Metis), because of the immigration of homesteaders to the Prairies (Staples 1974: 291).

In sum, as the evidence indicates, even in the pre-Calder era, the state did acknowledge that peoples it defined as "aboriginal" possessed something tangible that could be acquired through purchase. The treaties written in the period after Confederation also reveal the government's view of the nature of the entity that possessed this aboriginal interest. First, the terms suggest that the people had an economy based on hunting, fishing and trapping. Second, they seem to acknowledge that aboriginal societies contained a political component, for many undertakings of a social and political nature are included within the stated obligations of the aboriginal signatories. Finally, it appears that there is some recognition that the political component included a form of representative government, for the treaties are always signed by chiefs and headmen on behalf of both themselves and their constituents. However, the terms reveal that government perceived such societies to be transitory, for it was presumed that they would self-destruct as their members chose to take advantage of the benefits civilization provided. Given the wide range of societies incorporated within the same treaty provisions, it can be assumed that this image of peoples the government claimed were "aboriginal" was held to apply universally. One fundamental weakness of this policy (aside from its view of aboriginal peoples) was that its application was limited not to the class of peoples government defined as "aboriginal," but only to those peoples whose lands were required for settlement by colonists (and then only in instances where, unlike the situation in British Columbia, it would not confront existing colonial authorities to do so). The result was that, by 1969, there were still many places in Canada where treaties had yet to be signed.

CLAIMS POLICY AFTER THE CALDER CASE

On 31 January, 1973 the Supreme Court of Canada handed down its decision in the appeal of the Calder Case. As discussed in Chapter 4, the judgement held that the Nishga Indians had an aboriginal title to their lands at the time of contact with Europeans, but the vote split on the question of whether that aboriginal title still existed. As Prime Minister Trudeau remarked at the time, the case indicated that "perhaps" aboriginal peoples had more "legal rights" than his government had considered when they formulated the federal paper on Indian policy in 1969.

Although under no legal requirement to do so, the government decided to acknowledge the principle that aboriginal interests could still exist and on 8 August 1973, the Minister of Indian Affairs issued a policy directive consistent with that position. It averred (DIAND 1973):

> The present statement is concerned with claims and proposals for settlement of long-standing grievances. These claims come from groups of Indian people who have not entered into Treaty relationship with the Crown. They find this basis in what is variously described as 'Indian Title,' 'Aboriginal Title,' 'Original Title,' 'Native Title,' or 'Usufructuary Rights.' In essence, these claims relate to the loss of traditional use and occupancy in certain parts of Canada when Indian title was never extinguished by Treaty or superceded by law.

That is, it was intended to refer particularly to those groups recognized by the government as "aboriginal" with whom treaties were never signed.

Further, the statement acknowledged that "In all cases where traditional interest in land has not been formally dealt with, the government affirms its willingness to do so and accepts in principle that the loss and relinquishment of that interest ought to be compensated." It proposed that settlements be negotiated with "authorized representation" of each aboriginal group concerned. In short, the policy statement of 1973 represented a complete reversal of the position declared in 1969.

In the period since 1973, the government has consistently adhered to this policy, later termed the "Comprehensive Claims Policy." In particular, it has reaffirmed in statements issued in 1978 and 1981 its acknowledgement of the principle of unextinguished aboriginal interest and its willingness to negotiate settlements with native groups based on this principle. For example, it has agreed to undertake negotiations for claims advanced by groups in such diverse regions as Nova Scotia, Labrador, northern Quebec, the Northwest Territories, the Yukon Territory and British Columbia, and has made final agreements with the Cree of James Bay, the Naskapi of Schefferville and, in December of 1983, with the Committee on Original Peoples Entitlement (COPE) which represents the Inuvialuit (Inuit of the Western Arctic region of the Northwest Territories).

Yet, although the government has undertaken negotiations with native groups, it has yet to state publicly within the context of its "Comprehensive Claims Policy" what it perceives to be the content of aboriginal interests. However, the policy statements and the settlement documents provide sufficient contextual detail to be able to deduce the government's understanding of the acknowledged interests. An examination of this material is relevant, for, as I stated at the outset of this chapter, the interests that emerge are virtually identical to those the government is now proposing as aboriginal rights, to be entrenched in the constitution. The material can thus be used to provide an insight into how the government conceptualizes aboriginal rights and how it would define their continuity in the future.

THE NATIVE INTEREST: POST-CALDER

Initially, as the 1973 statement suggests, the government viewed the claims process as a means to provide compensation for a loss. This loss was described broadly as pertaining to "traditional use and occupancy of lands." Later, the government specified the nature of the loss within which compensation must be understood: "Claims are not only for money and land, but involve the loss of a way of life. Any settlement, therefore, must contribute positively to a lasting solution of cultural, social and economic problems that for too long have kept the Indian and Inuit people in a disadvantaged position within the larger Canadian society" (DIAND 1973). Clearly, then, in the view of the government, the aboriginal entity has lost its way of life, and the point of claims is to help find a means to resolve the cultural, social and economic problems resulting from the loss. In short, the statement reaffirms the gradual assimilation orientation of the pre-1969 government philosophy.

However, by 1978 the rhetoric changed. The purpose of claims was no longer "compensation" for the loss of a way of life, but rather, "to translate the concept of 'aboriginal interest' into concrete and lasting benefits in the context of contemporary society" (DIAND 1978: 5). And instead of promoting programs to ease the transition, the kinds of benefits to be included were: "lands; hunting, fishing and trapping rights; resource management; financial compensation; taxation; nature participation in government structure; and native implementation of the settlement itself" (ibid.). That is, benefits intended to maintain what the government perceived as an ongoing way of life.

This viewpoint is reaffirmed in the policy statement issued in 1981 (DIAND 1981: 7). It states that a primary objective of the claims is to "allow Native people to live in the way they wish." To this end,

> It is intended that these settlements will do much in the way of helping to protect and promote Indian and Inuit peoples' sense of identity. This identity goes far beyond the basic human needs of food, clothing and shelter. The Canadian government wishes to see its original people obtain satisfaction and from this blossom socially, culturally and economically.

And that in negotiations:

> The government intends that all aspects of aboriginal land rights are addressed on a local and regional basis. These aspects run the gamut of hunting, fishing and trapping, which are as much cultural as economic activities, to those more personal and communal ways of expression such as arts, crafts, language and customs. They also include provisions for meaningful participation in contemporary society and economic development on Native lands.

In short, the objective of the claims is to translate the aboriginal interest into particular benefits that will promote social, cultural and economic continuity of aboriginal society.

To ensure the economic aspects of this continuity through the claims process, the policy statement suggests that the traditional territory of the native people making claim be divided so that the larger share would be "owned" by Canada, and a smaller portion, selected from land "currently used and occupied," would constitute "Native lands." Further, on sections of these native lands, the aboriginal peoples would own sub-surface rights.

Measures pertaining to the maintenance of the traditional (hunting, fishing and trapping) economy would include the exclusive right to harvest all species on native lands, some species on Crown lands in the region and preferential harvesting rights for other species within the traditional region. In addition, the policy calls for "meaningful and influential Native involvement" on boards concerned with management and planning in areas of land use and wildlife. Finally, the document anticipates that a portion of native lands with sub-surface rights would be used to protect certain crucial wildlife areas, as well as community tracts, from disruptive development. However, "All areas, whether they include those for exclusive Native use or shared by the general public will continue to be subject to existing general laws as they apply to hunting, fishing and trapping; they will further be subject to present and future sound conservation policies and public safety measures" (*ibid.*: 24). That is, these administrative measures will be set out in a policy framework defined by government.

The policy statement is less forthcoming concerning the way benefits would act to promote participation in the dominant economy. But, it is clear on one point: the granting of sub-surface rights is intended, in part, "to provide Native people with the opportunity and incentive to participate in resource development." It also includes provisions respecting the incorporation of native-controlled corporations and financial compensation. Seen in the light of the stated reason for granting sub-surface rights, it would seem that these provisions are intended to provide a structure controlled by native people to develop these lands and the capital necessary to initiate the enterprise.

An examination of the terms contained in the final agreement signed in 1976 with the Cree and Inuit of the James Bay region of Northern Quebec and the agreement-in-principle reached in 1978 with the Inuit of the Western Arctic region in the Northwest Territories indicates a consistency with the kinds of provisions respecting lands and economy contained in the 1981 policy statement. The James Bay Agreement contains an additional provision. This settlement calls for cash incentives in the form of an income-security program, to be administered by the Quebec government, that is intended to encourage continued wildlife harvesting on the part of the Cree.

Certain provisions of the James Bay Agreement respecting the administration of services relating to justice, police, health, education and social services provide a more detailed insight into the government's perception of how the social and cultural aspects of aboriginal society will be maintained. The primary mechanism appears to be the creation of special jurisdictions that are mandated to operate in such a way as to honour Cree values, language and customs. Thus, in the area of judicial administration, procedural provisions must take into "consideration the particular circumstances of the district, the customs, usages and way of life." In education, measures stipulate, for example, the use of Cree in the classroom and Cree control over school boards and their areas of authority, such as the hiring of teachers and the institution of innovative curricula. However, as in the economic areas, the ultimate legislative authority for the administration of special jurisdictions in health, the judiciary and education lies in the hands of ministers of government rather than the aboriginal peoples themselves.

SUMMARY

In the government's view, the goal of the claims process in the post-Calder era is not to assimilate aboriginal peoples into Canadian society but rather to "allow Native people to live in the way they wish" (DIAND 1981: 7). A concept of collective continuity, which is termed both in the claims document and general policy as an "identity," is acknowledged and defined in a policy directive issued in 1975. This is expressed as follows (DIAND 1976: 1):

> The underlying assumption of this approach is that some degree of Indian status will continue, certainly as long as it is perceived as needed both by the Government and by people recognized as "Indian" under Canadian law. The Govern-

ment's relationship with the group recognized as Status
the establishment of reserves under the Indian Act, as in the
Indians is based on the concept of Indian identity within
Canadian society rather than on separation from Canadian
society or on assimilation into it.

In the context of the comprehensive claims policy, this "identity" is
seen as a result of the successful incorporation of strengthened traditional lifeways with "meaningful" participation in the lifeways of the
dominant society. To promote this goal, the government has proposed
to translate aboriginal interests into specific benefits. These include a
small land base owned by native people; harvesting rights; native
corporations intended to initiate economic development; representation on administrative boards concerned with land use and wildlife
management; the creation of special administrative jurisdictions in
which the language, customs and practices of the aboriginal population will be honoured; and control over education and other services.
In no instances, however, do the boards upon which aboriginal
representatives sit as members have senior legislative authority. This
fact, and the absence of any mention of the possibility of negotiating
ongoing political relationships with the Crown indicate that the
ultimate legislative authority is to remain in the hands of the federal
and/or provincial governments.

The federal government has often stated its reasons for opposing
legislative authority for aboriginal societies in claims negotiations.
One objection seems to dominate. It was perhaps stated most clearly in
the following government press release of the position taken in the
mid-1970s by the Dene Nation (then the Indian Brotherhood of the
Northwest Territories) and the Inuit Tapirisat of Canada (the group
representing the Inuit) in their land claims negotiations (Prime
Minister's Office 1977).

> In the Northwest Territories, the initial position put forward
> by the Indian Brotherhood and the Inuit Tapirisat ranges well
> beyond the policy the Federal Government is prepared to
> follow. As has been indicated, the Government has no wish to
> see the cohesion of ethnic communities undermined and
> quite the reverse. In the North, as in the South, the govern-
> ment supports cultural diversity as a necessary characteristic
> of Canada. However, political structure is something quite
> different. Legislative authority and governmental jurisdic-
> tion are not allocated in Canada on grounds that differentiate
> between the people on the basis of race. Authority is assigned
> to legislatures that are representative of all the people within
> any area on a basis of complete equality . . .

Accordingly, unless Indian and Inuit claimants are seeking the establishment of reserves under the Indian Act, as in the South, the government does not favour the creation in the North of new political divisions, with boundaries and governmental structures based essentially on distinctions of race and involving a direct relationship of the Federal government.

In other words, the federal government rejects the proposition that aboriginal rights include legislative authority to pass laws, for to incorporate such a provision would be inimicable to their view of democracy: the allocation of political authority on the basis of race.

The inclusion of a paragraph on reserves confirms this interpretation. Band councils do not have legislative authority. Rather, they operate on the basis of authority delegated to them by the federal government, which can thus veto laws passed by the councils or even enact legislation to change or cancel them without their approval. As is confirmed by an examination of the kinds of powers granted the Cree under the James Bay Agreement, it is this type of administrative power (one derived from delegated authority rather than legislative power) that the government has traditionally perceived as giving aboriginal peoples special political rights on the basis of race or ethnicity.

Initially, the federal government considered band councils to be transitional structures. However, in the period since 1973, it has accepted that such 'racial' governments can be permanent. But, until 1983, government always adhered to the view that band councils operated solely on the basis of delegated authority and hence under the jurisdiction of a legislature that was not organized on the basis of race. Now, it appears, a change is in the wind. In November of 1983, a House of Commons Special Committee on Indian Self-Government recommended eventual constitutional entrenchment of legislative authority for band governments in domains such as education, social services, taxation and other matters generally under the jurisdiction of provincial governments. To achieve this objective, the committee recommended the transfer of certain aspects of legislative authority from provincial and federal jurisdictions to bands and reserves. In effect, this would establish a third order of sovereign government in Canada. Given that this proposal advocates that band councils be elected solely by those Indians living on a reserve, it follows that by entrenching band-council powers, the federal government would be incorporating into Confederation the very 'racial' form of government it has so consistently rejected in the past! As the federal amendment proposed at the 1984 First Ministers' Conference attests (see Appendix J), it is a position government still seems reluctant to accept.

CONCLUSIONS: CURRENT POLICY AND ITS EVOLUTION

According to the statement cited at the beginning of this chapter, the federal government currently perceives aboriginal rights to include at least two fundamental characteristics: the right of aboriginal peoples to the "preservation and enhancement of their cultures" within Canada, and the right to "forms of self-government within the Constitution." These points are only vaguely described in this statement. But because they represent positions consistent with Comprehensive Claims Policy, I decided to discuss the provisions in this chapter. It is time to summarize these in relationship to a possible definition of aboriginal rights as it appears in the statement made at the March 1983 First Ministers' Conference.

With respect to cultural autonomy, if the logic of the claims policy is followed, government appears willing to accept that aboriginal peoples should be guaranteed certain important rights. These include, in particular, the power (1) to establish administrative regulations for education, health services and even judicial procedures within jurisdictions organized to insure control by aboriginal nations; (2) to continue the pursuit of subsistence activities such as hunting, fishing and trapping on their traditional lands; and (3) to participate in boards that administer such diverse economic matters as wildlife management and non-renewable resource-development on traditional lands.

With respect to political rights, government policy appears to suggest that legislative authority remain within federal and provincial jurisdictions. Thus, self-government would encompass mainly administrative matters (within the jurisdiction of senior government levels). Such an arrangement would provide aboriginal nations with what is known as "delegated" authority, which is the type of power presently used by municipalities in Canada. Indeed, government has often stated that this is the type of power it is willing to grant aboriginal nations. However, the matter of political rights may not rest at this point for long. One political body, the Special Committee on Indian Self-Government, has stated that band councils (and by implication other forms of aboriginal government) ought to be granted legislative authority for a wide range of matters. The question is whether this proposal will be taken further by governments in the future.

To what extent does the policy summarized here represent a change from the traditional government position on aboriginal rights? I would submit that the change is great. Prior to the Calder case, government regarded aboriginal rights as a transitional issue, for aboriginal societies would presumably assimilate eventually into the

Canadian mainstream. Given such an ideology, the notion that native peoples could possess permanent constitutional rights, including the perpetual right to self-government, was unthinkable. Immediately after the Calder decision, government took the position that the transition had already taken place. But within five years this was replaced by a new perspective: that aboriginal society is not a transitional phenomenon and its survival should be recognized. Initially, the political component of this continuity, based on legislative authority, was not to be entertained, but this also may be reconsidered. In sum, government policy on aboriginal rights has evolved, even on the question of political rights, from a position of resistance to one of reluctance.

In order to move beyond this point, one important matter must be clarified: whether or not, as is implied in the press release cited above, aboriginal political rights that include legislative authority are inimicable to liberal-democracy. If the answer is yes, then perhaps ethnic governments should not be considered at all, regardless of the abstract merits of the case. To this topic I now turn.

NOTES

1. One typical illustration, recorded in Chamberlin (1975: 120f), is the Delaware "walking purchase" of 1737. In that year, the Delaware Indians questioned the validity of a deed purchased by the Pennsylvania colonial government in 1686. They did acknowledge, with reluctance, that the deed was legal, for it had been signed by one element in the tribe (though not necessarily an element empowered to make such an agreement). However, they insisted that the tract remained undetermined, since its northern boundary was described as incorporating only lands "as far as a Man can go in one day and a half." The parties all agreed that the chief justice of Pennsylvania and a leading member of the Philadelphia community would make the determination of the precise boundary on behalf of all parties. These leading figures then proceeded to obtain the services of three fleet-footed woodsmen, who managed to cover a distance of 55 miles in the 18-hour period all parties had agreed was meant by a day and-a-half.

2. The geographical purview of the proclamation with respect to "Indian lands" is still a matter of some controversy. However, one point is certain. The proclamation is intended to apply to the land west of those acquired by the British through the Treaty of Paris. Thus, the eastern boundary of these lands would lie—in the southern part of the region—in the area west of the Alleghany Mountains and the Mississippi River. This was an area, according to Chamberlin (1975: 142-48), that had been set aside as "Indian country," as part of a policy to insure that colonial settlement went north into Quebec rather than west across the mountains. It was, parenthetically, a policy that created much dissatisfaction among the southern colonists, and is reputed to be a major cause of the American Revolution.

3. Although the belief that agriculture signalled civilization predominated, it was by no means universal. A contemporary view that counters this belief was expressed by Senator Frelinghuysen (1977: 6) during a Senate debate in 1830 on the removal of the Cherokee Indians of North Carolina:

> Mr. President: In light of natural law, can a reason for a distinction exist from the mode of enjoying that which is my own? If I use land for hunting, may another take it because he needs it for agriculture? I am aware that some writers have, by a system of artificial reasoning, endeavored to justify, or rather excuse, the encroachments made upon Indian territory and to denominate these abstractions the law of nations, and, in this ready way, the question is dispatched. Sir, as we read the sources of this law, we find its authority to depend upon either the conventions or common consent of nations. And when, permit me to inquire, were the Indian tribes ever consulted on the establishment of such a law? Whoever represented them or their interests in any congress of nations, to confer upon the public rules of intercourse and the proper foundation of dominion and property? The plain matter of fact is, that all these partial doctrines have resulted from the selfish plans and pursuits of more enlightened nations; and it is not matter for any great wonder, that they should so largely partake of a mercenary and encroaching spirit in regard to the claims of the Indians.

6

ABORIGINAL RIGHTS IN THE CONTEXT OF CANADIAN DEMOCRACY

As shown in the previous chapter, governments, both at the federal and provincial levels, although prepared to acknowledge that aboriginal nations should have some kind of self-government, appear reluctant to grant them final legislative authority. There are a number of possible explanations for government reticence. Many of these concern practical matters, such as the costs involved, which could be resolved were governments willing to act on the principle. Other reasons, such as the possible fear that entrenchment might lead ethnic groups to make similar demands, are quite complex for they involve perceptions that may or may not prove true. Still, were the desire to act in favour of entrenchment present, arguments could easily be made to differentiate the circumstances of aboriginal peoples from those of all other Canadians. Possibly, as well, government reticence is due to a belief that the aboriginal case lacks merit. However, with aboriginal rights already in the constitution, and with the current impasse centred on how to entrench aboriginal political rights, it seems rather late in the day to expect such a position to hold much moral weight (although its political impact on a public that is unaware of the federal position on claims or of recent court decisions is a factor to be weighted by politicians).

The federal government has, however, generated one argument that could challenge the case for entrenchment of legislative authority on merit alone. It is the argument that entrenchment of legislative authority would violate the fundamental tenets of liberal-democracy upon which Canadian society rests. Therefore, any government that wishes to uphold these values must avoid jeopardizing them, regardless of the merits of the aboriginal nations' case. Perhaps best identified as the "civil rights" or, as Weaver (1983) puts it, the "ideological" problem, the argument has been raised constantly by government. Indeed, Weaver (ibid.: 89f) places it as the first of a number of concerns that government representatives have expressed on the subject. In particular, she suggests this objection reflects "the liberal-democratic ideology which assigns significance to equality, individualism and freedom from discrimination on the basis of race, religion, nationality, etc. Hence for the government, aboriginal rights demands become problematic because these demands call for unique treatment by government . . ."

This ideological problem was bluntly expressed in a report written by the Eighth Legislative Assembly of the Northwest Territories (1976) in response to a draft proposal on Dene self-government:

> (Some) people think that much of the Territories should be converted into racial states along ethnic lines . . . If you're for (this), then you've got to support something that has always been abhorrent to Canadians and violates our history— separating people according to race. Frankly, support (this) and you have to support South Africa and its policy of apartheid—separate development for each of its founding races. The fanciful name for it is 'positive' racism. And it's well known for what the free world thinks of South Africa for it.

If this argument is true, then the case of the aboriginal nations does not stand a chance, for it seems inconceivable that Canadians at this time in history would agree to an action that would undermine their established political values. Indeed, seen in this light, the notion of entrenching municipal levels of government and guaranteed seats on boards based on aboriginal ethnicity alone must be viewed as a compromise that represents an important accommodation to principle.

In this chapter, I shall discuss this so-called civil rights or ideological issue in detail. I do so for two reasons. First, as the above discussion indicates, I believe this is the strongest argument advanced against entrenchment and so it must be laid to rest if further progress is to be made in defining the nature of political rights within the constitution. My second reason is practical. As should become apparent, a detailed examination of the issue provides a context within which the various proposals concerning the entrenchment of aboriginal political rights can be better understood.

SOME CHARACTERISTICS OF LIBERAL-DEMOCRACY

Without belaboring the point, it can be stated that, if nothing else, a liberal-democracy is a system of democratic government in which the value of individual freedom is joined through a political and legal structure to a belief in the legitimacy of majority rule (MacPherson 1977: 3). Crucial to the self-image of such a state is the notion that the system of government should operate to maximize equality (Pennock 1950). This doctrine, according to Pennock, is manifested both in the equality of treatment within the legal system and with respect to judgements made concerning claims by individuals. With regard to this latter point, which Pennock calls "the equality of consideration," he states that "in considering the respective claims of two individuals we should treat them alike, equally, in the absence of some relevant basis for distinction" (*ibid.*: 82 f). Although it does not often work in practice, the intent of this type of ideology is to insure that all persons, regardless of differences in class and race, are given equal treatment by the state.

Modern liberal-democracies, of course, contain many provisions that allow equality of consideration to be shaped in favour of one group over another. Usually, for example with clauses protecting Blacks and women in the United States, the objective is to counter previous discrimination that left such groups disadvantaged in comparison to the mainstream. Like the gradual-assimilation approach of the treaties, these are conceptualized as temporary measures that will be rescinded once their objective to promote true equality of consideration has been achieved. Similar thoughts are present, even in contemporary times, when rights for aboriginal peoples are considered, as the provisions in the 1969 federal Indian policy attest.

The case for aboriginal rights, particularly the entrenchment of political rights, differs significantly from this view of special rights within a liberal-democracy. First, they are to be permanent features of Canadian polity. This means that they will continue to exist even if the special disadvantages perceived to exist among Canadian aboriginal peoples were overcome, or if aboriginal peoples as a class ultimately found themselves in an advantaged position vis-à-vis the Canadian mainstream. Second, they are to be political rights rather than rights pertaining to the social or economic spheres. Indeed, it is these facts, more than the idea of granting special status alone, that are central to the argument under consideration here. In short, the question to be addressed is whether the granting of permanent political rights to a special class of citizens (rather than special rights on a temporary basis) is possible within an ideology that maintains the principle of equality of consideration.

The key to the resolution of the issue lies first in the mechanism by which liberal-democratic states incorporate their citizens. According to anthropologist M.G. Smith, there are two ways by which this can be attained. The most common, founded on what he calls "universalism," is based on the precept that the ethnonational rights of sub-national entities will have no official recognition in the state. This leads to a type of liberal-democracy where "the regime is inherently assimilative in orientation and effect. By assimilating all its members uniformly as citizens, it fosters their assimilation in other spheres also, notably language, connubium, economy, education and recreation" (Smith 1969: 435).

This system of incorporation is well exemplified by the United

States. In that country, the principle of universalism is strong and hence the designation of special political rights is perceived to be inherently contradictory to the notion of the equality of consideration. Thus, the provision of schools that were supposed to give "separate but equal" treatment to white and Black children was considered to be based on unequality and was thus rejected as unconstitutional by the U.S. Supreme Court. Canada, it is clear, has traditionally presented an equally strong universalistic approach to the question of granting native peoples special political rights on the basis of their aboriginal status.

Smith describes his second type of liberal-democracy as "consociational." In this form of incorporation, the nation-state explicitly acknowledges that it is composed of members who share different linguistic, cultural or ethnonational traditions. It provides mechanisms that help guarantee their survival rather than assimilate them to a common norm. Equality of consideration, then, is reconciled by identifying areas of jurisdiction, such as education, within which a universalistic theory of incorporation will apply only within segmental boundaries. Here, "separate but equal" is not considered antithetical to democratic ideals, as long as there really is equality. The primary example of such a state formation is Belgium, which has explicitly entrenched the segmental rights of the Dutch and French populations in its constitution (Senelle 1978).

In addition to these two classical forms of incorporation identified by Smith, there is a third type of liberal-democracy, representing a compromise position between the two. In such a nation-state, citizenship is avowedly incorporated on the basis of complete universalism. However, the state provides consociational institutions that are used to accommodate segmental political rights, albeit in an oblique manner. The prime example of this form of government is Switzerland's, which accommodates four ethnonational entities: the Germans, the French, the Italians and Romansh. In such a nation-state, the principle of equality of consideration is always manifestly universalistic. However, in reality, means are found to limit its application in a manner that insures segmental control.

ETHNONATIONAL POLITICAL RIGHTS IN BELGIUM AND SWITZERLAND

The description and analysis of consociational democracies has been the subject of numerous studies by political scientists. The principal investigator is Arend Lijphart who, independently of Smith, coined the term consociation to identify a set of political institutions and style of political leadership characteristic of certain forms of plural democracy (Lijphart: 1977). Lijphart's work has focussed primarily on the discovery of mechanisms that account for the political stability evidenced in certain consociational democracies. He finds that the crucial factor in maintaining stability is the cooperation of ethno-national elites in the governance of the state—a conclusion that has been criticized by scholars such as Schmid (1981) and Steiner and Doerff (1980).

A complete exposition of Lijphart's position would of necessity incorporate some of this criticism. However, my objective here is more limited. I intend to focus solely on the question of how nation-states, based on the tenets of liberal-democracy, mould their political institutions in a manner that can accommodate the political rights of their ethnonational entities. This is a matter which, judging from the political science literature, is not in dispute. Therefore, I rely more than would normally be appropriate on the work of a single individual—Lijphart's—and in particular on his *Democracy in Plural Societies*, for this book is the clearest and most detailed description of this aspect of consociational democracy.

One must begin any such discussion by stating that in most respects, all three forms of liberal-democracy are identical in terms of institutions and basic political values; that is, all have elected governments, parliaments, court systems and charters that protect individual rights. For example, in both Belgium and Switzerland, as in Canada and the United States, constitutional provisions guarantee such rights as the equality of all individuals before the law; freedom of speech, assembly and the press; democratic elections; and, in a few cases, even free education. Of particular importance is protection against discrimination.

Thus, in general terms, democracies that entrench ethnonational political rights follow Smith's assertion (1969: 434) that "although in such systems citizenship presumes identification with one or the other of the primary ethnonational collectivities, formally at least no differences in civil status in the common public domain attach to membership in any of them, since each bears coordinate status." These democracies differ from strongly universalistic states only with respect to the inclusion of specific provisions guaranteeing the protection of the special interests of the various segments incorporated within the state. Lijphart (1977: 25) classifies these special features into four fundamental institutions and values: the grand-coalition style of government; the principle of proportionality in parliament and the civil service; segmental autonomy in political matters; and the mutual veto or concurrent majority rule with respect to constitutional changes. A comparison of the ways in which these principles are realized in Belgium and Switzerland should illustrate the differences between the direct and the indirect forms of consociation, respectively. To this we now turn.

The primary structural feature of democracies that entrench ethno-national rights is the incorporation of provisions to insure that these entities retain autonomy in the operation of their own affairs. This is accomplished in both types of consociation by dividing matters into those of common concern, which are decided through processes that equally incorporate all citizens, and matters that are of concern primarily to the separate segments. The latter concerns are generally limited in scope to core institutions relating to the retention and the development of each segment's particular way of life. They are mandated to be decided by a constituency composed of members of the particular segment.

The direct system, as exemplified in Belgium, provides a straight-forward means to achieve this end. This country is organized as a unitary state, which has a single national parliament vested with legislative authority. Most matters are decided by the national parliament itself; however, explicit areas of jurisdiction are controlled by regional, linguistic and cultural councils, each of which is intended explicitly to serve the particular ethnonational entities identified in the constitution under Article 1b. Key delegations of authority pertain to matters such as the designation of the official language of a district (Article 3b), cultural control over education and autonomy in other cultural matters that include even some aspects of international relations within the cultural realm (Article 59b).

In indirect systems, segmental autonomy is attained without explicit constitutional recognition of ethnonational entities or their powers. Rather, it is accomplished through the intervention of a mediating institution, which is manifestly intended for another purpose. Typically, this is a federal-type structure in which legislative authority is divided between a central (or federal) and regional governments that have sovereignty over matters of most concern to segmental autonomy. It is a system that, as Lijphart points out (*ibid.*: 42), works best when "each segment is concentrated and separated from the other segments or to put it differently, a society in which segmental cleavages coincide with regional cleavages." That is, the system works well when the territorial divisions are created in a manner that insures that ethnonational entities can establish their legitimacy through the intervention of the principle of majority rule.

In Switzerland, this form of segmental autonomy is achieved through the operation of a federal structure that divides political authority between a central federal government and regional governments called cantons and half-cantons. Both cantons and half-cantons, and within them communes (or municipal-level governments), have exclusive legislative authority in a wide range of domains, including language, education, culture, and civil and criminal justice (Sauser-Hall 1946: 7f). Indeed, within this highly autonomous system, the federal constitution stipulates that, as long as its structure is democratic in nature and does not discriminate between Swiss cantons and other cantons, each canton is free to create the form of government its citizens desire.[1]

Of particular note is the following observation on Swiss federalism and the protection of ethnonational rights, made by Carol Schmid (1981: 28 f): "the purpose of the federal structure is to protect linguistic and cultural minorities. However, most institutions are not aimed primarily at giving protection to minorities against majorities. Rather, they are the pillars of the Swiss Federal System and their minority protecting functions are a fortuitous bi-product." This orientation well exemplifies the "equality of consideration" typical of those consociational systems overtly organized on the principle of universalism.

The second essential feature of democratic systems that entrench ethnonational political rights is the inclusion of mechanisms to insure "each segment a complete guarantee of political protection" (Lijphart 1977: 36 f). This is generally done through one of two procedures, by which ethnonational entities can block legislation that would adversely affect their interests and powers: the mutual veto, in which each segment has the right to stop such legislation, or the concurrent majority rule, in which all the segments must agree by a majority vote of its members to enact changes (ibid.: 25).

In the case of Belgium, this protection is accorded directly to the Dutch-speaking and French-speaking entities by means of explicit constitutional provisions concerning amendment. The system, as will be indicated below, operates in a restricted sphere of legislation, for, fundamentally, the constitution of Belgium considers nation-state to be a single, united entity with supreme legislative authority vested in a central parliament. Members of this parliament are deemed by its constitution to be representatives of the Belgian nation-state as a whole, and are directed under Article 32 to "represent the nation and not merely the province or subdivision of a province which elected them" (Senelle 1978: 352).

As is true of any constitution, Belgium's provides a means to alter existing structural arrangements. Generally speaking, these procedures, although extraordinary in themselves, do not explicitly accommodate the interests of the ethnonational segments. However, under the constitution, as was mentioned above, a certain domain of legislation has been delegated to bodies composed of and elected by the members of each of the constitutionally recognized ethnonational entities contained within the Belgian nation-state. In the case of any legislative or constitutional change that would alter these arrangements, a set of procedures intended to protect segmental autonomy are invoked. The first, found in Article 32b, is that "the elected members of each House (of parliament) are divided into a French-language group under Dutch-language groups. . . ." (*ibid.*: 352). The second, which clearly follows the double majority method of veto, is the manner in which such votes are counted. Typical are the provisions dealing with changes that would affect provincial boundaries and the division of Belgium into linguistic regions. These, as Article 1 states, can only be altered as follows (Senelle 1978: 349): "Such an act must be passed by a majority vote in each linguistic group of each of the Houses, on condition that the majority of the members of each group is present and that the total number of votes in favour of each of the two linguistic groups attains two-thirds of the votes cast."

The constitutional protection of segmental autonomy in nation-states that are manifestly universalistic is more complex than that in direct systems. In Switzerland, for example, the process is organized around a complicated majority formula based, first, on the acceptance of cantons and half-cantons as central units. In particular, the Swiss constitution is altered primarily through a popular referendum. According to this procedure, in order to be successful in this forum an amendment must pass with two kinds of majorities. The first is based on a popular vote taken on a nation-wide basis. The second must include majorities in a majority of the twenty-six cantons and half-cantons (Schmid 1981: 40). Thus, an amendment could be blocked even if a minority of the population voted against it, provided that when examined from the point of view of the second test, the total comprised a majority of votes in a majority of cantons.

The procedure is cumbersome and offers no guarantee for the protection of segmental interests. The reason for this is that the proportion of German speakers to the population as a whole is large enough that they could insure the adoption of any amendment in their own ethnonational interests (Schmid: 1981: 39). However, the system works primarily because Switzerland is also divided by at least two other important cleavages: between Roman Catholics and Protestants, on the one hand, and between the centre and periphery, on the other. This situation has resulted in a recurrent tendency for the Roman Catholic cantons of French and Italian Switzerland to combine with German-speaking Catholics to oppose any amendments "they feel to be either too centralizing or threatening to cantonal autonomy." Schmid concludes (*ibid.*: 40): "Although the referendum process is not a device for minority recognition as such, its operation has often enabled the religious and linguistic minorities to combine for structural reasons as a defensive measure against the Protestant German, economically strong 'center'."

The last two features of consociational democracies are proportionality in representation among the segments and the adoption of a grand-coalition style of government (as opposed to a government-opposition style). Both provisions are intended to insure that, whatever the outcome of an election, all ethnonational entities will be represented within both the national parliament and the government itself. In both Belgium and Switzerland, this is accomplished either directly through measures such as that in the Belgian constitution, which distributes membership in the cabinet equally between French and Dutch speakers (Senelle 1978: 361); or indirectly through a provision such as that in the Swiss constitution which limits membership in federal cabinets to a single representative from any one canton (Schmid 1981: 39).

ETHNONATIONAL POLITICAL RIGHTS IN CANADA

It is clear from the above that accommodation can be achieved within liberal-democratic ideologies. The question is whether it is possible to do so within the framework of the Canadian state. The answer is yes.

Although Canada is said to be a strongly universalistic state with respect to the accommodation of the aboriginal fact, a different picture emerges in relation to the French fact. Here, all politicians readily acknowledge that the country is structured to accommodate two primary segments. The French-speakers or francophones comprise 30 per cent of the total population, the majority of whom live in the province of Quebec. It is a grouping, which Lijphart suggests (1977: 102), represents a classic example of a segment in a plural society. The second grouping, which is often glossed as English-speaking or anglophone, does not conform to the homogeneous entity implicit in the term "segment." Rather, it is only a segment in a "residual sense" (*ibid.*). Better described as "non-French," this grouping which is widely heterogenous ethnically, comprises the remaining 70 per cent of the population, forming the majority in the remaining nine provinces and two territories of Canada. According to this definition, then, "aboriginal peoples," in terms of their political rights, belong to the population labelled here as "non-French."

The question of how well Canadian political institutions accommodate the French fact has been a controversial issue since the inception of this country. Many, such as those members of the French segment who wish to see Quebec leave Confederation and those non-French who seek to force their assimilation would say, not well at all. However, the success of accommodation is not at issue here; rather, it is whether any accommodation exists at all, for to hear politicians' remarks about aboriginal self-government one might be led to believe that the entire idea was foreign to Canadian political thought! Yet, it is obvious that, in the face of the French fact, the structure of the Canadian state, unlike that of the United States, is organized in the belief that it can accommodate ethnonational political rights. It is to provide a basis for comparing this perceived accommodation with the specific proposals advanced by aboriginal organizations (discussed in the next chapter), and not to evaluate their effectiveness in achieving ethnonational accommodation, that I examine the provisions for the French fact contained in the Canadian constitution.

Canada, clearly, does not use a direct form of consociation as does Belgium. Rather, like Switzerland, it relies on an indirect system that is compatible with an ideology of universalism. The keys to segmental autonomy in such systems are the creation of mediating institutions on a regional basis that are manifestly intended for another purpose, and the concentration of ethnonational populations within certain of these regional jurisdictions. That is, "because government at the subnational level is in practice always organized along territorial lines, federalism offers an especially attractive way of implementing the idea of segmental autonomy" (Lijphart 1977: 42f). In Switzerland, the regional unit is the canton; in Canada, it is the province. In short, Canada's form of consociation is based on, first of all, the creation of provincial jurisdictions, which happen to be organized in such a way that one of them, Quebec, contains the majority of the French-speaking population.

Under the terms of the Constitution Act, 1867 (formerly known as the British North America Act) and the Constitution Act, 1982, the French segment, because it forms a majority in the provincial jurisdiction of Quebec, gains legislative authority over a broad domain of powers in that region. These include the administration of justice, including court procedures; the ability to raise moneys through direct taxation of its residents and through borrowing; and the designation of French as an official and public language in the province. As well, on the basis of provincial authority, Quebec retains primary control over education, provided only that this mandate is carried out in accordance with certain universal guarantees contained in the federal constitution. Finally, under Section 6(2) of the new constitution, citizens are expressly guaranteed the right to move freely within, and to take up residence in any locale, in Canada. Provincial governments can pass legislation restricting such migration if the law has "as its object the amelioration in a province of conditions of individuals in that province who are socially and economically disadvantaged if the rate of unemployment in that province is below the rate of unemployment in Canada" (Section 6(4) Constitution Act, 1982). Such a provision is an indirect means of stemming population flow in situations where a segment believes its autonomy could be undermined by a shift in population mix.

Segmental autonomy in Canada is also accommodated on a non-territorial basis. Again, as they are written, the guarantees apply to segments only indirectly. The first of these non-territorial guarantees pertains to official languages, which, according to Sections 16, 19 and 20 of the 1982 act, are English and French. As a consequence of this provision, individuals—be they members of either segment—have the right to communicate with the federal government and in the federal courts throughout Canada in either language.

The second non-territorial guarantee pertains to "minority language education" (Section 23). This provision allows parents, where numbers warrant, to educate their children in the official language spoken by the minority population of the province in which they reside. Although, on the surface, this guarantee seems to be couched in a universalistic theory of incorporation, it is not. Two restrictions are mentioned. The first is that the parent must be a Canadian citizen; the second (and from the point of view of ethnonational division, the more critical) states that the right is limited to the first language (spoken or in which educated) of the parent. Thus, an English-speaking parent can demand his child be educated in English in any province. However, English-speaking parents cannot demand that their child be educated in French when, as is the case in Alberta, it is the official language of a minority of the population. In such a situation, this right is accorded only to francophones. By restricting access to minority language education in this manner, the constitution is implying that there are two segments—the French and the English—whose rights are to be protected on the "separate but equal" rationale characteristic of direct forms of consociation.

The second essential feature of segmental autonomy is the ability of the ethnonational entities to protect themselves from imposed changes that would adversely affect their autonomy. As stated above, in a 'true' consociation these mechanisms are generally organized in a manner that enables the segment to block passage of such legislation through a veto or a double-majority procedure. Because the French segment comprises only 30 per cent of the population, such an arrangement would be an important measure to guarantee the autonomy of the French segment in the Canadian state. And, as is well known to students of Canadian history, it was the inability to establish an amending formula that could accommodate this objective within the ideology of universalism and majority-rule that was the primary reason behind the delay in patriation of the constitution until 1982.

In the end, the constitution was patriated with an amending formula that, in principle, appears to accomplish these twin objectives. Specifically, the amending procedure in Section 38 contains two mechanisms. The first does not accommodate any segmental concern. The second, however, states that any amendment to the constitution that "derogates from the legislative powers, the proprietary rights or any other rights or privileges of the legislature of government of a Province . . . shall not have effect in a province the legislative assembly of which has expressed its dissent thereto by resolution supported by a majority of its members prior to the issue of the proclamation to which the amendment relates" (Clause 3). Thus, it is possible for Quebec (or any other province) to invoke this provision in order to block the effect of a constitutional change within the territory under its political jurisdiction.

This formula, one must hasten to add, is flawed by the fact that it was incorporated over the objections of the Quebec government. However, an examination of the evidence leads to the conclusion that the objections did not flow primarily from a disagreement with the principle of opting out itself. Rather, they flow from a belief that without such compensation, a time could come when the Quebec government would be forced by financial circumstances to accede to constitutional changes, which, on purely political grounds, it would reject (Milne 1982: 152). It is a fear that is anticipated in the constitution: Section 40 suggests that in cases where the transfer of powers from the provincial legislatures to the federal Parliament relate to "education and other cultural matters," compensation will be paid to those provinces that opt out. However, this accommodation has not removed Quebec's opposition to the amending formula as a whole.

Regardless of Quebec's objections concerning the practical consequences of the formula entrenched, opting out is an important mechanism for resolving the problem of reconciling the ideas of universalism and majority-rule to those requirements for segmental protection that are essential for consociational incorporation to work. Thus, again, Canada has followed the Swiss example and protected segmental autonomy tacitly, through the introduction of an intermediate institution: the province. However, unlike the Swiss canton, a province has two ways to act: it can combine with other provinces to block constitutional change; or it can act alone, not to veto the amendment for the others, but rather to block its intrusion into its sphere of jurisdiction. In this regard, it seems to me that Canada comes closer to entrenching the political protections characteristic of consociational incorporation as defined by Smith than does Switzerland—a nation-state that is viewed, and views itself, as an archetypal example of a consociational society.

Canada, according to Lijphart's analysis (1977: 125-27), also exhibits features of the proportionality principle. The clearest example is contained in the convention that three of the nine Supreme Court justices must be from the province of Quebec. As well, proportionality in representation in Parliament is attained through the creation of riding demographics, which results in a situation where, in 75 per cent of the ridings, the proportion of the French or the non-French component is at least 90 per cent. This means that representatives in certain ridings will always find themselves voted in by members of the French-speaking population. Finally, statistics indicate that the introduction of French as an official language has created a situation in which the proportion of French speakers in the civil service has grown to the level proportionate to their numbers in the population (*ibid.*).

The weakest element of ethnonational accommodation in the Canadian system relates to style of government. Canada is avowedly majoritarian in philosophy and hence basically subscribes to the winner-take-all government-opposition image characteristic of such universalistic systems as the United States and Great Britain. Indeed, as McRae aptly points out (1974: 301), it is the majoritarian philosophy more than any other factor that thwarts true accommodation of the French fact.

Nonetheless, Canada is not devoid of features to accommodate the French-speaking population regarding style of government. Most important is the fact that, because of the division of powers, provincial authorities often work in close cooperation with federal officials in order to resolve problems of mutual concern. Quebec, because of its status as a province, thus becomes an essential partner in the process of consensus-building. Accommodation is also found within the federal structure itself and most conspicuously in the tradition that the positions of governor-general (at least since it was Canadianized), the speaker of the House of Commons and the chief justice of the Canadian Supreme Court are to be alternated between the two segments. Finally, there is the tacit agreement that federal cabinets ought to contain members from all provinces, and certainly every attempt is made to include francophones from Quebec.

In sum, although few would deny that Canada has a political system that is based on principles of universalism in citizen incorporation, it does contain features of segmental accommodation. These manifest themselves particularly with respect to the protection of segmental autonomy, through the establishment of provincial spheres of jurisdiction and provisions that enable provinces to opt out of imposed changes that could adversely affect their power to protect segmental rights. Finally, although present to a much smaller degree, Canadian democracy also exhibits features of proportionality and the grand-coalition style of government. As this evidence shows, it would be wrong to draw an analogy between Canada and the United States. Canada, rather, is like Switzerland: a nation-state that conforms to an intermediate form of consociational accommodation.

CONCLUSIONS

The federal government and the representatives of the aboriginal nations agree that some form of aboriginal self-government should be entrenched in the constitution. The primary issue in dispute at this juncture is the nature of its authority. Representatives of aboriginal nations, on one hand, argue that since their rights are based on self-determination, these powers (whatever their scope of jurisdiction) should be sovereign, in the sense of having final legislative authority. Government (and here it is presumed that provincial governments are included), on the other hand, suggest that these be delegated powers, such as those granted to municipalities. This would mean that, ultimately, decisions that were opposed by the respective jurisdictions with final legislative authority—the provincial and federal governments—could alter or block them unilaterally. It is a proposition that has not met with much favour among aboriginal leaders.

Over the years the federal government has stated quite strongly that it must oppose the entrenchment of sovereign aboriginal political rights, for not to do so would violate fundamental values of liberal-democracy. Seen in this light, their proposals for municipal levels of government and for seats on administrative boards on an ethnic basis seem quite generous, since they represent an important accommodation of these principles. This attitude is not limited to government alone.

However, as the evidence presented in this chapter shows, the fears of the federal government are unfounded. It is possible, as in Belgium and Switzerland, to accommodate within a single nation-state both ethnonational political rights (including legislative authority or its equivalent over certain matters) and the fundamental value-orientation of liberal-democratic rule. Indeed, as ought to have been clear to the legislators who made these pronouncements against the entrenchment of legislative authority for aboriginal governments, many structures within the Canadian state are perceived to attempt just such an accommodation with respect to the French fact. Thus, if one accepts the aboriginal nations' case on its merits, there can be no objection to the extension of similar provisions to accommodate the aboriginal fact, and no need to present municipal government as a reasonable compromise. The main question, then, is whether the specific proposals advanced by the aboriginal leaders at the March

1983 First Ministers' Conference are of a type that can be accommodated within the context of liberal-democratic values. This is the subject of the next chapter.

NOTES

1. In fact, according to Sauser-Hall (1946: 144-50), cantons vary regarding their democratic form. Some use a system of direct democracy, in which the legislative assembly drafts legislation that is enacted only after it has been passed by the people as a whole, while others use a mixed form in which referenda are used as a check on the legislative authority of the cantonal assembly.

7
From Theory to Practice

As discussed in the previous chapter, the example of the Belgian and Swiss types of consociation can prove quite useful in countering government objections to the entrenchment of aboriginal self-government on ideological grounds. However, if the type of compromise consociation calls for is unacceptable to the aboriginal nations, then its adoption would have little practical value in resolving the issue. The fact is that there is no unanimity among aboriginal nations regarding the appropriateness of adopting a consociational form of accommodation with the Canadian state. To some, such as those represented by the Coalition of First Nations, the compromise does not seem to present a workable solution. Indeed, for some groups, the very inclusion of an aboriginal rights clause in the constitution is suspect. As Bill Two River, a Mohawk chief, put it, "With one swipe of the pen, they are committing genocide on Indians by making them Canadian citizens" (*Edmonton Journal*, 27 October 1983). This view is shared by others, such as some member nations of the Indian Association of Alberta.

Nevertheless, those aboriginal representatives present at the March 1983 First Ministers' Conference agreed that accommodation of their political rights could be effected within the framework of Confederation (see Chapter 3). According to Dr. Ahenakew (1983), national chief of the Assembly of First Nations, "We recognize that it is the view of many that the word 'sovereignty' defines an extreme at one end of a list of options available and the word 'assimilation' describes an extreme on the opposite end. We say there is a 'middle ground'." This middle ground, as it was described by the representatives, was said to include a division of responsibilities between a national and a segmental level; a land base upon which to establish the legislative authority deemed essential to insure the autonomous development of the segment; the protection of segmental rights through the introduction of a veto over changes that otherwise might be imposed by the other segments of the population; and some degree of proportionality in representation. As such, it is a position that reflects in its specific goals, as well as in its overall orientation, consistency with the principles of consociation discussed in Chapter 6. Thus, in principle, there is every reason to believe that the kind of political power advocated by the middle-ground approach and belonging within the definition of aboriginal rights could be reconciled to the kind of consociational arrangements that exist within Canada.

In this chapter, I focus solely on a description of those proposals that advocate the middle-ground or consociational approach. I do so for two reasons. First, this approach does, in fact, represent the position advanced by most aboriginal nations that have brought forward specific proposals. And second, because of the nature of their stance, such proposals seem to represent solutions that could easily be incorporated without further objection in principle: for, in fact, they are merely alternatives to the provisions now in place for the (intended) accommodation of the French fact.

Among the aboriginal organizations that have adopted the middle-ground approach, there are two distinct kinds of proposals concerning the details of the consociational arrangements. The first kind is advanced primarily by those aboriginal groups that reside in the southern part of Canada and in the Yukon.[1] It is found equally in both Indian and Metis proposals and is supported, at least in part, by the recommendations contained in the House of Commons Special Committee Report on Indian Self-Government. The second type is advocated primarily by the native groups that reside in the Northwest Territories, in particular by the Dene, Metis and Inuit regional organizations. It finds support in statements made by the Government of the Northwest Territories—the political jurisdiction mandated by Ottawa to function as a provincial-type legislative authority in the region. It is best to outline the elements of each separately and then to return to a discussion of common issues.

THE SOUTHERN APPROACH

Although those aboriginal organizations representing nations that reside in the southern part of Canada and in the Yukon have produced a large number of individual proposals, in effect they all adhere to one basic model. Since this is illustrated in the findings of the House Committee on Indian Self-Government, I shall rely mainly on its report for this discussion.

In essence, this approach to entrenchment of rights advocates the use of the direct method of consociation. That is, the ethnonational political rights of the aboriginal peoples would be specified and guaranteed to a named ethnonational entity: the aboriginal peoples of Canada. As such, it is similar, in its overall philosophy, to the classical approach to consociation exemplified in the Belgian constitution.

Although certain political rights are expected to be acquired on a non-territorial basis, the fundamental emphasis in all proposals is on self-government within particular territorial jurisdictions. These domains are generally perceived to be parcels of land that are geographically encapsulated within existing provincial territories. The archetypal example of this land base is the reserve.

Indeed, the existing reserve system does comprise one important component of the proposed solution. These lands now total approximately 10,000 square miles and contain a population of over 200,000 individuals. Collectively, this represents an area roughly five times that of Prince Edward Island and a population that is twice as large. However, for the plan to work, additional territory will be required to accommodate the perhaps 500,000 Indians and Metis who do not have a recognized land base upon which to transfer legislative authority, and those Indian peoples who live on reserves that are of insufficient size and/or economic potential to make them viable. Hence, the proposals do not call for the retention of the status quo but advocate the transfer of additional lands presently under the control of provincial and federal authorities. This issue was clearly perceived by the Special Committee of the House of Commons (1983: 112): "Canada has set aside 130,168 km^2 for national parks, yet only 26,335 km^2 for Indian reserves. The Committee does not dispute the need for parks, defence bases and airports; but surely the land rights of the aboriginal inhabitants of this continent deserve as much or more attention." It is a position that may imply that some park lands should be turned over to aboriginal peoples.

According to the southern model, these reserve territories must acquire, through some form of direct entrenchment, the legislative authority deemed necessary to protect and develop aboriginal ways of life. That is, as the Metis National Council (1983: 1) put it, they must have "jurisdiction over political, cultural, economic and social affairs and institutions deemed necessary to their survival and development as a distinct people."

Included within the scope of these powers would be some constitutionally held by the provinces and federal government, particularly in areas such as education, social services, policing, financing and economic development. In addition, the proposals seek a joint relationship with the federal government concerning matters of international relations with other aboriginal nations and some additional control over family law, in general, and child welfare, in particular. As well, the proposals of many organizations advocate proportionality in representation both in the federal parliament and provincial legislatures by means of a guaranteed number of directly elected seats.[2]

The range of ethnonational traditions encompassing those aboriginal peoples who live in the southern part of Canada and in the Yukon is quite broad. Hence, it is anticipated that whereas the powers to be acquired through entrenchment will be specified, different groups will shape their institutions of government in different ways. That is (House of Commons 1983: 56),

> As Indian people begin to plan their systems of government, it can . . . be expected that a wide variety of governmental styles will emerge. These styles will reflect historical and traditional values, location, size, culture, economy and a host of other factors. This diversity is to be respected.
>
> It can be expected that several . . . governments may wish to combine for various purposes—administrative, economic or cultural. Examples would be education associations, economic development corporations, tribal councils, treaty organizations and assemblies.

Thus, this model envisions a situation in which the forms of governments will be plural not only ethnonationally but also structurally. For example, government may operate in the manner depicted in the following citation from the Commons report (ibid.: 13):

> The Iroquois (as they were known by the French) or Six Nations (as the English called them) or the Haudenosaunee (People of the Longhouse, as they called themselves) have a formalized constitution, which is recited every five years by elders who have committed it to memory. It provides for a democratic system in which each extended family selects a senior female leader and a senior male leader to speak on its behalf in their respective councils. Debates on matters of common concern are held according to strict rules that allow consensus to be reached in an efficient manner, thus ensuring that the community remains unified. A code of laws, generally expressed in positive admonitions rather than negative prohibitions, governs both official and civil behaviour. Laws are passed by a bicameral legislature, made up of senior and junior houses. A council of elders oversees the general course of affairs. Since officials are chosen from each extended family, the system is called 'hereditary.' While the commonly held belief is that hereditary chiefs hold dictatorial powers, these leaders are actually subject to close control by their people and can be removed from office by them.

The southern approach calls for the protection of legislative powers in these territories through a direct form of veto, which is similar in concept, though perhaps will not be in form, to the approach used in Belgium. Again, in line with the idea of direct consociation, the constituency of aboriginal governments will not follow the universalistic orientation characteristic of Canadian democracy. Rather, the plan might incorporate only those individuals whose standing has been determined to be ethnonationally appropriate for participation. In other words, persons who do not belong to the ethnonational group but live on a reserve or reserve-like jurisdiction may not be given the power to influence government directly (as through elections), regardless of their term of residence. It will thus be a private form of government in the sense that the constituency will not be open to Canadian citizens on the basis of universalistic criteria. It is with respect to this latter point that the approach may well find its toughest opposition— a matter to which I shall return later.

The Approach of the Northwest Territories

The approach taken in the south (and it would appear in the Yukon) is modelled on the idea that aboriginal peoples form a small fraction of the total regional population and that, as a rule, they reside on small territories encapsulated by non-native residents and provincial lands. In the Northwest Territories circumstances are different, and so is the vision.

The Northwest Territories is a vast jurisdiction that covers a land mass of over 1,200,000 square miles or roughly one-third of the total territory of Canada, but comprises a very small population, which in 1981 numbered only 47,000. Of these, at least 58 per cent (census questionnaire) were classified as "native" people. Politically, the Northwest Territories is a non-self-governing region with ultimate legislative authority vested in the federal government. However, it is an accepted fact that this region, like the Yukon Territory to the west, will ultimately achieve provincial status and thus acquire all the sovereign legislative powers contained in Sections 92 and 93 of the Constitution Act, 1867, and the control over immigration (under certain economic conditions) as set out in the Constitution Act, 1982.

Proposals that have been accepted, in principle, by the federal government call for the eventual division of the Northwest Territories into two political jurisdictions, each of which, it is assumed, will become a self-governing province. One of these jurisdictions, provisionally named "Nunavut," would be created out of the eastern portion of the Territories. This is the homeland of a sizeable portion of Canadian Inuit, who would comprise the majority of the proposed new province's population of 17,000. The second, provisionally called "Denendeh," would be created primarily out of the western portion of the Territories. Home to most of the members of the Dene Nation, it has a population mix that, depending on how the figures are derived, contains a majority or near majority of native people among its population of 30,000.

The approach to the establishment of aboriginal political rights in the Northwest Territories is based on the following facts: first, unlike the south, the region as a whole is only thinly populated; second, the sole land-users in the major portion of the territory are the native peoples; third, the native component of the population in each of the two proposed new provinces has a majority or near-majority status; and fourth, at present, government in the region does not have legislative authority, but is, in effect, a colony of the federal government.

Given these conditions, the issue of political rights for aboriginal peoples cannot easily be separated from the evolution of sovereign government for the Northwest Territories and, indeed, at the most basic level the two become intimately intertwined. The result is that, in contrast to the direct approach taken in the south, organizations in the Northwest Territories tend to stress entrenchment through the indirect means exemplified by Switzerland.

The central feature of this method in Canada, as it was discussed in Chapter 6, is the division of legislative authority between federal and provincial levels of government. Thus, proposals in both regions tend to emphasize the fundamental assertion made by the Nunavut Constitutional Forum (1983: 1), a body composed of Inuit and non-Inuit members empowered by the Government of the Northwest Territories to examine pathways to self-government:

> Nunavut is 'public government'. That is, it is a government for all the people who live in the area embraced by Nunavut whether they were born in Igloolik or Trois Rivières, Lloydminster or Yellowknife. Nunavut is not a government only for Inuit, but a government firmly founded on the Canadian political tradition of public services and the power of participation for all people who live in a geographical area.

That is, as the document goes on to state: "Nunavut is not an ethnic government" (p. 5). But it is, nonetheless, a government that will "provide specific guarantees for Inuit in respect of certain of their vital interests" (p. 1), for "Nunavut will not only be a provincial-type government, but also the homeland of the distinct and ancient Inuit culture. It has a special role in protecting the heritage of all Inuit because it will be a government with the powers and resources to do so" (p. 7). In short, the approach advocated for both Nunavut and Denendeh is to entrench the rights of the aboriginal peoples of the region not because they are aboriginal peoples *per se*, but also because they hold majority or near-majority status in the jurisdiction.

Whereas all of the proposals advanced for Nunavut and Denendeh agree completely on this fundamental approach to entrenchment, there is much variation among them with respect to specific details. In order to indicate this range, I shall discuss two proposals. The first concerns political evolution in Nunavut, which has been tabled by the Nunavut Constitutional Forum. The second, proposed by the Dene Nation and the Metis Association of the Northwest Territories, is serving as one model for self-government currently under consideration by the Western Constitutional Forum (a body equivalent in form and function to the Nunavut Constitutional Forum and empowered to make recommendations concerning the constitutional evolution of Denendeh).

NUNAVUT: THE PERSPECTIVE OF THE NUNAVUT CONSTITUTIONAL FORUM

The proposal tabled by the Nunavut Constitutional Forum (1983) envisions a form of government which parallels that existing in established provinces. Generally, the powers that the proposal intends Nunavut to acquire are those found under Sections 92 and 93 of the Constitution Act, 1867. However, there are exceptions, of which one is a proposition concerning international relations. Here, because of the interests of the Inuit in interacting with other Inuit who live in different nation-states, the proposal recommends that the Nunavut government, because of the majority status of the Inuit in its jurisdiction, "be recognized as having legitimate interests in various international matters and that a Nunavut constitution specify that in cooperation with the Government of Canada it may undertake such international activities as may be agreed from time to time with that Government" (p. 35). This proposition is similar in intent to the kinds of arrangements that enable Quebec to participate in international forums related to francophone issues.

According to the proposal of the Nunavut Constitutional Forum, the institutions of government would resemble those found in existing provinces. As in these jurisdictions, legislative authority would be vested in a legislative assembly, to be called the Nunavut Assembly (p. 11) and composed of twenty-five members. Four of these are to be elected from each of the four regions of Nunavut, and the remaining nine on the basis of population (p. 12). However, it is recommended that provision be made to accommodate small isolated areas (such as the Belcher Islands) that are acknowledged to have a significant degree of homogeneity. However, the proposal does not explicitly agree to decentralizing political decision-making by vesting certain domains of legislative authority in sub-provincial (that is, regional) governments. In fact, in their only detailed statement on the subject, the Nunavut report argues that the Western Arctic Regional Municipality (WARM)—a self-governing jurisdiction proposed by the Inuvialuit—be given only delegated authority; that is, the proposal would structure government for the Inuvialuit on a basis similar to that granted the Cree under the James Bay Agreement.

In sum, despite some differences, the Government of Nunavut, as it is perceived in this proposal, would be essentially like any other Canadian province in terms of the scope of its powers and its organizational structure. The accommodation of the segmental rights of the Inuit, like those of Quebec, would thus flow only from the manner in which the content of these powers and structures are shaped.

DENENDEH: THE PERSPECTIVE OF THE DENE NATION AND THE METIS ASSOCIATION

Denendeh, as it is proposed by the Dene Nation and the Metis Association of the Northwest Territories (1982), is intended to be a "political system that embod[ies] Dene values (and) reflect[s] Dene style and form of political organizations" (1982: 5) within a structure of public government for the region. In contrast to the Nunavut proposal outlined above, however, Denendeh government would acquire certain powers and contain certain structures that would easily distinguish it from any other provincial jurisdiction.

Denendeh powers would be "province-like" in that the government would have legislative jurisdiction in all matters that are now provincial responsibilities under Sections 92 and 93 of the Constitution Act, 1867. As well, akin to the Nunavut proposition, it is argued that Denendeh should establish a shared arrangement with the Government of Canada to enable it to enter into agreements with other aboriginal nations.

However, the proposal goes well beyond these kinds of powers to advocate sole legislative authority in areas seen to be crucial to the protection and development of the Dene way of life. For example, it is argued that in the areas of navigation and fisheries, presently under federal jurisdiction, Denendeh must gain powers "necessary to ensure protection of the aquatic environment of Denendeh which is basic to our traditional Dene way of life," as well as control over aspects of employment and labour legislation in order "to preserve and develop historical Dene work styles and employment relations . . ." (p. 7).

Structurally, the government of Denendeh would be "province-like," in that it would have a legislative assembly (called the National Assembly of Denendeh) with ultimate responsibility for Denendeh-wide policies and a community or municipal level of government (called "community government"). As well, it is implied, although there is room for interpretation, that the division of powers would resemble that of the existing provinces in that legislative authority would be vested solely in the National Assembly, and community government control would therefore be exercised only through delegated or subordinate authority. That is, "policies, laws and programs of one community which affect other communities must be consistent with Denendeh-wide policies as determined by the National Assembly of Denendeh" (p. 14).

But the government of Denendeh would be unlike provincial governments in other respects. One, which parallels and develops an idea proposed for Nunavut, is the entrenchment of matters such as official languages within the constitution of the jurisdiction. In Denendeh, this would be accomplished through the establishment of a Charter of Founding Principles. This document would spell out certain fundamental matters, which all persons who wished to participate in the political life of Denendeh would have to acknowledge. Key provisions of this proposed charter would include, in addition to the entrenchment of the native languages of the region as official languages, guarantees to protect fundamental human rights of all citizens, as they are outlined in the International Covenant on Civil and Political Rights (to which Canada is a signatory), and the right of the Dene (and other citizens) to "establish government funded institutions and services to reflect their respective values and ways" in areas such as education, health services and social services (p. 9). This latter point is of some importance for it indicates a desire to shape not only the content but the structure of government in order to promote Dene institutions and values.

Similar proposals are made with respect to the internal organization of government institutions themselves. For example, community councils, which are delegated the administrative powers for local jurisdictions, would resemble band (or reserve) governments in that they would be composed of a chief and councillors. However, participation in their election would be by all residents in the community— regardless of their ethno-affiliation with the Dene segment. It is also proposed that the National Assembly be composed as a council of all local chiefs, or a combination of chiefs and directly elected representatives rather than the simple riding system of election that is typical of other provinces.

The key institutional feature intended to promote Dene institutions and values in Denendeh is contained in the decision-making process, itself. Rather than the elected representative model that is currently used, the Dene Nation and the Metis Association of the Northwest Territories propose to "encourage government by the people. Instruments through which people could not only be consulted but really be a part of the decision on major policies would be the right of all people" (p. 6). The concept upon which this is to be based is that of consensus (as opposed to the strict government-opposition style characteristic of majoritarian systems). Consensus is defined as follows (p. 21f):

> The consensus style of decision-making involves a lot more than the absence of political parties. Things are not that simple. There are many single party or no party states in the world where there is no consensus just as there are many multiparty states where there is no real democracy. Consensus begins with a respect for one's own rights and assuming the responsibility to achieve these rights. Therefore, the limits on the amount of responsibility and authority that can be delegated to others is very real. Alongside the respect for one's own rights there must be a respect for the rights of others.

To achieve a consensus style, discussion must replace debate:

> Discussion, underpinned by the concept of a respect for rights and recognition that differences are a fact of life, makes it possible for everyone to contribute, to share, to learn, and on this basis, reach decisions. There may, and likely will, be disagreements but the changes of disagreements reaching discord and open hostility are minimized because, if nothing else, people will at least have [an] understanding of the reasons why people decide to do certain things.

The way in which consensus would be reached would be through the process of direct democracy. For example, at the community-government level, the primary governing body would not be a council composed of elected officials, but rather a community assembly, which would meet regularly to make decisions on the following kinds of matters (p. 14):

(i) those by-laws, programs, services and institutions required to meet . . . community needs;
(ii) [which] people [will] sit on a Community Council to implement community programs and run community institutions;
(iii) which issues require majority vote in a referendum before legislation is implemented by the Community Council.

The referendum process would also be significant in shaping consensus at the level of the National Assembly. Here, in addition to the limitations placed on its authority by the division of powers and the necessity to conform to the Charter of Founding Principles, there is the requirement that "legislation dealing with certain subjects within the legislative competence and jurisdiction of the Government of Denendeh will be submitted to the people of Denendeh for referendum and the legislation may only be passed if a majority of electors agree to it" (p. 15).

Finally, in order to protect the position of the Dene and their aboriginal rights, the proposal calls for two provisions that correspond to the direct entrenchment method used in Belgium. The first is a minimum guarantee of 30 per cent of the seats on community councils and the National Assembly, should the Dene population ever fall below that percentage. The second is the introduction of a second chamber at the provincial level. Called the Denendeh Senate, this institution would be composed entirely of Dene. It would have the power to veto any legislation adopted by the National Assembly or community councils, should it determine that this would "adversely affect aboriginal rights" (p. 17). The function of the senate in this regard would be to outline its objections and then re-examine and vote upon revisions made to the legislation.

In sum, Denendeh, as envisioned by the Dene Nation and the Metis Association of the Northwest Territories, differs from the Nunavut proposal in two fundamental respects. First, it would shape structure and powers, as well as the content of legislation to enhance the traditions and values of the aboriginal peoples within its jurisdiction. Second, it would protect the aboriginal rights of the people through both direct and indirect means. Nonetheless, both approaches share the same underlying orientation toward entrenchment. Fundamentally, in both Denendeh and Nunavut, political rights are to be protected, indirectly, through the structure of the public government of the region and not directly, as in the southern approach, through the creation of separate, autonomous and hence private governments.

The key to the success of this approach, then, is the ability of the ethnonational segment to control the institutions of public government tacitly and for reasons manifestly not associated with their ethnonational status *per se*. The essential requirement, in Canada as in Switzerland, is a majority (or near-majority) status of the segment within an acknowledged provincial (or regional) jurisdiction. This element is recognized by the Dene, Metis and Inuit peoples, and methods for insuring its continuity have been proposed. These, in themselves, as the discussion below will indicate, can give rise to difficulties that might make the public government approach harder to achieve.

RECONCILING THE PROPOSALS WITH
CANADIAN POLITICAL IDEOLOGY

Consociation, as outlined in the Canadian constitution, is based on the ability of an ethnonational segment to control public institutions through its majority status within a political jurisdiction. As a result, it presents an option that allows for segmental accommodation within a political ideology that is avowedly universalistic and hence does not admit to ethnonational distinctions. Universalism and majority-rule, then, are the twin pillars upon which this method of consociation is founded. As will be discussed below, neither the southern nor the Northwest-Territories approach completely meshes with these requirements, for each confronts one of these pillars directly. Thus, a solution to the entrenchment of the political rights of the aboriginal nations requires a resolution of this confrontation.

The southern approach advocates the explicit entrenchment of polical rights and hence the establishment of a third order of sovereign government based on an ethnonationally segmented constituency. In reality there is nothing inherently inimicable in this process to the tenets of liberal-democracy (as discussed in Chapter 6). Still, it seems to give the impression that there is. For example, columnist Don McGillivray may be the first of many to condemn the orientation proposed by the House of Commons Special Committee Report as "apartheid" and to argue that (*Edmonton Journal*, 12 November 1983):

> The treatment of Indians in Canada already has racist aspects, of course. But to harden these into constitutional law makes the problem permanent. A serious matter such as the establishment of postage-stamp provinces here and there on a racially segregated basis should be honestly debated. Indians deserve better than apartheid. They deserve the full rights and privileges of Canadians, as citizens, not by meeting a racial test.

What the southern approach proposes is, of course, not apartheid.[3] Rather, it is the classical form of consociation. Both consociational and apartheid types of state organization are superficially similar in that each explicitly acknowledges the existence of separate segments. Where they differ, however, is in the method by which citizens are incorporated. As Smith points out (1969: 435), apartheid states are not organized on a consociational basis but rather on the principle of "differential incorporation." This is a system in which state institutions are structured in a manner that provides differential access to power and resources among the various ethnonational segments. Thus, unlike a consociation, the system based on differential incorporation entrenches inequality among the segments. South Africa, for example, is a state that practises differential incorporation. Here, unlike Belgium, there is no attempt to create a power-sharing arrangement within a common parliamentary structure; no willingness to distribute power or material resources on an equitable basis; no agreement that segmental autonomy will exist for all segments; and, most crucially, no provision to insure that each segment in the plural society can block legislation perceived to be in conflict with its vital interests.

Without such guarantees, the fundamental tenets of liberal-democracy cannot be said to be present within the ideology of apartheid states. Thus, the evidence shows that, contrary to McGillivray's claim, racism as an institutionalized aspect of state organization results not merely from an acknowledgement of the existence of ethnonational groups; rather, it arises when the state, having recognized that such entities are present, makes no provision to insure that the ethnonational entities can interact with each other on a fair and equitable basis. There is, then, no "equality of consideration." Hence, the argument that the entrenchment of special political rights for aboriginal peoples would necessarily introduce a racist element into Canadian democracy is simply false.

Instead of 'apartheid', I would label what is being proposed in the southern approach as 'apartness'—a state that is as accommodatable within classical consociational forms as it is understandable, given the strong assimilative pressures the majority has placed on aboriginal peoples (especially in the south) over the past century and more. Yet, those who argue 'apartheid' when they mean 'apartness' are touching on a fundamental cultural point. The Canadian tradition of segmental accommodation, at least since Confederation,[4] has not been organized on the basis of segmental autonomy as in the classical Belgian system. We have, rather, relied on the formula based on universalism. It is an ideological orientation that does not accept apartness or segmentation along ethnonational lines as a legitimate basis for governmental organization. As a result, the southern proposal directly contradicts certain fundamental perceptions that many Canadians believe can provide the only means by which ethnonational political rights should be accommodated.

For this reason, it is all the more important to acknowledge the apparent acceptance of this method by the Commons committee. Their attitude may, in fact, signal to Canadians that an exception should be made in the case of aboriginal peoples. It is a message that, it is hoped, will gain wider acceptance as the inherently democratic nature of the proposals becomes known to a larger public.

The approach developed in the Northwest Territories studiously avoids confronting this problem. This is due, not least, to the fact that earlier proposals that advocated entrenchment along the lines now proposed in the south (although for areas much larger than reserves!) met with the kind of negative response contained in the press release (cited in Chapter 5). As a result, groups in the Northwest Territories decided upon the use of the indirect approach, discussed above. It is a method that, in Canada, requires that aboriginal nations gain a majority (or near-majority) standing within recognized provincial boundaries. And, it is with regard to retaining such majorities that these proposals find their most serious difficulties with existing ideology.

It is true that, were Denendeh and Nunavut to be created soon, at the moment of their inception both would contain majorities of aboriginal peoples. However, in absolute terms, the native component of the population in each jurisdiction is exceedingly small (about 15,000 Inuit in Nunavut and about 15,000 Dene and Metis in Denendeh). As a result, one can easily foresee the development of conditions where, through the immigration of non-native people, the native component could become reduced to a small minority. In such an event, under the system of majority-rule, their ability to protect segmental rights indirectly through the control of Denendeh and Nunavut institutions of public government would be greatly reduced, or even eliminated.[5]

Of course, when the unemployment rate in the region is higher than the national average, it is possible to stall immigration by invoking Section 6(2) of the Constitution Act, 1982. However, although statistics on current unemployment show a higher rate than the national average, the economic potential of the region is high, and it can easily be predicted that over the course of the next few years, the pressure to develop the resources of the two new provinces will be great. Hence, the existing constitutional formula would not protect a change in the population mix of the region.

Since this problem is recognized by the proponents of segmental autonomy for Denendeh and Nunavut, their proposals for the development of public government in both jurisdictions have incorporated procedures to protect the aboriginal populations from losing control over their segmental autonomy. For Denendeh, these mechanisms include factors of a direct consociational nature, of which examples are the Senate, the entrenchment of ethnonational guarantees in the Charter of Founding Principles, the guarantee of a minimum of 30 per cent of the seats in governmental bodies, and the ownership of Dene lands that would not be subject to expropriation. In the view of the Nunavut Constitutional Forum, Nunavut would protect Inuktitut (the language of the Inuit) in a similar fashion.

In the end, however, all proposals for Nunavut and Denendeh rely primarily on an indirect procedure that would control the institutions of public government through the maintenance of a majority hold on the electoral process. In particular, these proposals advocate an electoral procedure that would enable native peoples to control the voting, even if their populations fell below the majority status. The central element in this solution is the residency requirement for voting. Instead of the six months or one year that is customary, the Nunavut Forum calls for a three-year requirement in Nunavut, whereas the Dene Nation and the Metis Association require a ten-year residency.

The advocacy of this proposition is based on two related observations. The first is that economic development in the North usually attracts migrants who are looking for immediate financial gain and hence tend to spend only one or two years in the region. The second is the observation that non-native peoples with long experience in the North frequently tend to be in fundamental agreement with the segmental objectives of the aboriginal peoples who live there. Thus, the argument goes, if the residence rule for voting were fixed at a period longer than the conventional six months or one year, there would be a better chance that the majority of the electorate would remain sympathetic to and supportive of the political rights of aboriginal peoples, regardless of its ethnic composition. It is clearly a procedure that, in principle, would conform well to the public government–universalistic orientation of the Northwest Territories approach as a whole.

One basic difficulty with this option is that, although it is universalistic and therefore maintains a sense of equality of consideration, it can be perceived by some to be unfair. For example, the *Globe and Mail* (16 August 1983), in an editorial on political development in Nunavut, picked out the three-year residency proposal as a "problem." It stated, "the authors endorse a three-year residency before people in Nunavut can vote, contrary to the franchise guaranteed to all citizens in the Charter of Rights." It went on to say, in another related matter, that "making second-class residents of other Canadians is certainly unreasonable." Whether such provisions as a three-, five- or even ten-year residency requirement for voting is contrary to the Canadian Charter of Rights is perhaps a question that only the courts can ultimately resolve.

However, the perception that this course of action is somehow inimicable to the tenet of fairness, like the view that direct consociation inevitably produces apartheid, does not bear close scrutiny. The indirect solution to ethnonational political accommodation requires majority control. Given the demographic profile of the Northwest Territories, it would be impossible for the long-term residents (of whom the native people form the majority) to gain majority status without a longer-term-residency requirement than is the norm at present. The blunt fact is that if a short-term residency requirement were in place, majority status would rest in the hands of transients, many of whom come to the region without families and most of whom do not intend to remain for a long period. In other words, a short-term residency requirement would create a situation unique in Canada: a province in which those persons with the least commitment to the jurisdiction and its people would have legislative control. Clearly, then, in the Northwest Territories the franchise question will inevitably produce a perception of unfairness from the vantage point of a particular group. Seen in this light, it seems obvious that a system that tilts the balance in favour of long-term residents over transients is not an unreasonable one to advocate.

CONCLUSIONS

Those aboriginal nations that seek a middle ground are proposing constitutional recognition of the kinds of powers that are quite consistent with liberal-democratic rule. However, it is true that each of the two methods proposed does vary to some extent with existing political practice. Yet, both the direct-consociation proposal of the southern approach and the longer residency requirement in the Northwest Territories are undertaken for the soundest of reasons: entrenchment could not work without them. Furthermore, although they are foreign to our traditional political culture, neither seems to produce a situation that is at variance with fundamental democratic values. Surely, therefore, it would be possible for Canada to incorporate a direct system of consociation and longer residency requirements with regard to its native peoples, if the alternative is to block any accommodation of their political rights. In short, all that entrenchment would require is a degree of flexibility in organizing institutions of government. It hardly seems a high price to pay.

But to accept the position of native peoples is to take a chance. Their proposals are not devoid of problems, and it is certain that some of these will prove major obstacles to progress in the future. Not least, it is likely that some of the aboriginal nations will not be satisfied with the kinds of arrangements being proposed by the advocates of the middle-ground approach. Thus, government acceptance of these propositions may only lead to the furthering of political divisions among aboriginal nations similar to the current situation in the French segment.

There may be many reasons not to take the chance, and, despite its rhetoric on the merits of the case, the government seems intent upon seizing on every reason to delay action.[6]

What, then, is the argument in favour of swift action? In the first place, delay is not without costs to the aboriginal nations, particularly to those peoples who have proposed the middle-ground compromise, and to those non-native Canadians who wish to see the issue resolved. But most crucial is the cost to Canada itself. For over one hundred years, Confederation has been incomplete, for it has been organized without the recognition of the special political standing of the aboriginal nations. With patriation of the Constitution, including a clause on aboriginal rights, Canada took an important step to rectify this situation. But without the entrenchment of the political rights of native peoples, Confederation is still incomplete. At the March 1983 First Ministers' Conference, the aboriginal nations represented, produced a set of proposals that would round out this aspect of Confederation in a manner most amenable to the existing political value system of Canada. These proposals, as I hope to have shown in this chapter, although not entirely free of potential problems, have been carefully thought out.

Given that the aboriginal nations have an unassailable claim to special political rights, as the evidence from ethnology and history as well as from legal and political precedent demonstrates, what is crucial to note is the moderate stance of the solutions proposed. They indicate, above all else, that these nations still seek an answer that is mutually satisfactory to all concerned. As one Dene leader once remarked to me: "While others are trying to negotiate their way out of Confederation, we are trying to negotiate our way in." Their position reflects a faith in Canadian institutions that, under the circumstances, is truly remarkable. Now, while Canadians are thinking through the implications of a new constitution, and while dialogue on aboriginal rights is underway, is surely the best time for government to return the faith native peoples have shown in Canadian democracy and take the chance they offer to complete Confederation.[7]

NOTES

1. The Council for Yukon Indians has not explicitly stated how it would entrench its constitutional political rights. However, it is likely that the Yukon aboriginal peoples would use a model similar to that advocated in the south.

2. The scope of powers found in Sections 92 and 93 of the Constitution Act, 1867, are virtually identical to that which band councils now have under Indian Act legislation (see Appendix D). The main difference is that band councils function on the basis of delegated authority (see Chapter 5). Therefore, at least for some aboriginal nations, the creation of self-governing bodies responsible for matters of education, health, and the administration of justice would only require that Parliament pass legislation to transform the current form of authority to one of sovereignty. It

is a proposition that has been favourably considered in the Report of the Special Committee on Indian Self-Government (1983). With respect to proportionality, the Report of the Metis and Non-Status Indian Constitutional Review Committee recommended that 18 seats in the House of Commons be assigned directly to native peoples (1981: 39). As well, the Alberta Federation of Metis Settlements advocates, in addition to guaranteed seats, the creation of a special "Aboriginal Peoples Court" with jurisdiction to adjudicate matters that pertain to aboriginal rights (1982: 19). However, the AFN position does not specify proportional representation or special courts.

3. For a discussion of this point with respect to northern claims, see Dacks (1981: 78).

4. In the period from 1840 until Confederation in 1867, Canada had a direct consociational system informally in place. During that period, Canada was governed under the Union Act which created a United Province out of English-speaking Upper Canada and French-speaking Lower Canada (Dawson 1970: 15). Although this arrangement was intended to fulfill Lord Durham's objective of assimilating French Canada to the language and values of the British settlers, it was soon recognized that this orientation would not work. As a result, government in this period closely followed certain features that are characteristic of the classical consociational systems, even after the devolution to responsible government in 1848. One was proportional representation. Under the Union Act of 1840, Upper and Lower Canada were each given 42 members even though Lower Canada had a higher population. The intention of this provision was originally directed toward fostering assimilation. However, as Ormsby states (1974: 271), "Once assimilation was rejected, equal representation assumed the guise of a political guarantee for the continued existence of two distinct cultures." This could be sustained through the use of an informal system of "double majorities" being required to pass certain legislation (Lijphart 1977: 125).

Another feature of consociation was the development of politics based on the "Grand Coalition." This was accomplished through (1) the development of a system of "double prime ministerships and twinned ministerial portfolios which were carefully balanced to give equal weight to the eastern and western sections of the United Province"; (2) loose coalition alliances between the Lower Canada *Blues* and the Upper Canada Conservatives and the Lower Canada *Rouges* and the Upper Canada Reformers; and (3) the rotation of the political capital of the United Province between Upper and Lower Canada (McRae 1974: 255).

However, the consociational arrangements did not include provisions for a true "veto" by either segment, nor did they insure cooperation among segments for the passage of legislation. The result was "immobilization and deadlock" (*ibid.*: 256), which led to a new "federal" system known as Confederation. There were a number of factors "which favoured a federal Union, but the predominant federal influence was the dual character of the Canada's. Confederation was an impossibility without the concurrence of French Canadians and the concurrence was forthcoming only when guarantees for its institutions, language, laws and religion had been spelled out in resolutions that were to form the basis for the British North America" (Ormsby 1974: 274).

5. The concern over such an eventuality is not completely hypothetical, having already occurred in Canadian history. When Manitoba entered Confederation in 1871, it contained a population of a little over 12,000. Of this total, 82% were Metis, 6% Indian and only 14% non-native. The majority of the Metis was French speaking (Staples 1974: 290). Institutional arrangements incorporated into the Manitoba Act included special provisions regarding anglophone and francophone rights. Among these were: equal rights of usage of the French and English languages in the legislative assembly and the courts and, most significantly, an Upper House, which was to be "ethnically balanced" (McRae 1974: 256). Indeed, similar provisions to guarantee both French and English as official languages were to be extended to those portions of the Northwest Territories that were to become Saskatchewan and Alberta. Thus, McRae concludes (1974: 256): "Briefly, for two decades after Confederation there lingered the possibility of a second—or perhaps even a third—province of the Canadian federation which would incorporate in its institutions the principle of cultural duality according to the model of Quebec."

   The demise of this possibility took place only 20 years later with the repeal of provisions to secure French segmental protection by the Manitoba legislature. This action can be correlated to a shift in demographics. Between 1871 and 1886, the Manitoba population increased by 97,000 to a total of 109,000. Of this number, the percentage of those of "British," "English," "Canadian" or "anglophone" background was 70%. The native Indian component of the population was 5% and the francophone component (including 6% francophone of Metis origin) was only 10%. In short, aboriginal population had been swamped by a vast immigration in the province of non-francophone, non-aboriginal groups (Staples 1974: 291). For a detailed account of the impact of this immigration on the Metis, see the report of the Metis and Non-Status Indian Constitutional Review Committee (1981: 51-68).

6. One issue that is bound to be brought up is whether a nation-state that organizes around the liberal-democratic ideal of majority-rule ought to consider the accommodation of special political rights of a small minority. The aboriginal peoples comprise the fourth-largest ancestral-origin group in Canada. However, they are not concentrated in any one geographical area, nor, at roughly 4% of the total population, do they constitute a number that necessarily warrants political accommodation. Why, then, should such a numerically small group of people be granted special political rights?

   The argument against supporting such rights was phrased most concisely by Canada's premier politician of the past quarter century, Pierre Elliot Trudeau. In 1968, he wrote that "politics cannot take into account what might have been" (1968: 9), a view he justified later in the following pointed way (*ibid.*: 31):

Historical origins are less important than people generally think, the proof being that neither Eskimo nor Indian dialects have any kind of privileged position. On the other hand, if there were six million people living in Canada whose mother tongue was Ukrainian, it is likely that this language would establish itself as forcefully as French. In terms of *realpolitik*, French and English are equal in Canada because each of the linguistic groups have the power to break the country. And this power cannot yet be claimed by the Iroquois, the Eskimos or the Ukrainians.

It is this argument, states Weaver (1981: 55), that lay at the heart of the government's rationale for instituting the termination policy in 1969. It is also the argument, along with the issue of costs, that is advanced whenever policy matters relating to minority rights are under discussion.

Given the majoritarian orientation of Canadian political culture, a counter-argument seems much more difficult to make. In the abstract, however, surely the philosophical counter must suggest that the relative size and/or power of a group have nothing to do with the recognition by the state of the legitimacy of its claim. Attention must remain fixed only on the legitimacy of the claim itself.

In the case of aboriginal rights this test has been successfully passed: first by the court decision in the Calder case, then by explicit government policy, and finally by their entrenchment in the Canadian constitution. Thus, whatever the merits of the abstract argument against the majoritarian stance asserted by Trudeau, one point is established. Regarding aboriginal rights, Trudeau's assessment is incorrect. They are not "might have beens" and their legitimacy, therefore, persists independently of the size of the aboriginal population. The example of Switzerland supports this view.

The Italian cantons, even though they comprise only 4% of the total population, are accorded ethnonational political rights equivalent to those of the French cantons. Switzerland also recognizes the rights of the Romansh, the original people of the country. They number only 1% of the total Swiss population (Schmid 1980: 16), but they have the same rights in their communes as do the Italians in their cantons. Finally, the Swiss state, rather than promoting an assimilationist attitude, has taken special measures, including the provision of special funds, to foster the "preservation and furtherance of the cultural and linguistic individuality of regions in which Romansh and Italian are used" (*ibid.*: 24).

The lesson is obvious: the native population of this country is not too small to protect.

7. In March 1984, the second First Ministers' Conference on Aboriginal Rights was held. At this meeting, the federal government proposed a constitutional accord entitled "Commitments Relating to Aboriginal Peoples of Canada" (for full text see Appendix K). This document states that "aboriginal peoples of Canada have the right to self-governing institutions. . . ." It is an idea that was supported by the provinces of Manitoba, Ontario and New Brunswick. It was opposed by the other

provinces, primarily because the accord lacked clarity with regard to the meaning of "self-government."

From the early reports emanating from the conference, one might be led to believe that at least the federal government and the three provinces that supported the idea had already agreed to the kind of offer advanced by the aboriginal peoples and described in this book. Had this been the case, then surely a great advance would have been made. Unfortunately, such an interpretation is erroneous. A detailed examination of the proposed amendment shows clearly that the federal government has not strayed from its view that aboriginal governments must derive power through delegated authority (see Chapter 5), for the constitutional accord says that whatever commitment is made must be read as not "altering the legislative authority of Parliament or of the provincial legislatures, or the rights of any of these with respect to the exercise of legislative authority." This is contrary to the view expressed by the aboriginal nations at both conferences: that their governments must have legislative jurisdiction over matters within their domain.

The primary substantive difference, then, between the federal government's position at the 1983 conference and the current view is that now both it and three provinces are prepared to bind themselves to the status quo through a constitutional accord. This degree of progress seems too limited, in my view, to be considered a significant advance toward completing Confederation.

APPENDIX A

CONSTITUTION ACT, 1982

The Canada Gazette, Part III, 21 September 1982.

25. The guarantee in this Charter of certain rights and freedoms shall not be construed so as to abrogate or derogate from any aboriginal, treaty or other rights or freedoms that pertain to the aboriginal peoples of Canada including

(*a*) any rights or freedoms that have been recognized by the Royal Proclamation of October 7, 1763; and

(*b*) any rights or freedoms that may be acquired by the aboriginal peoples of Canada by way of land claims settlement.

PART II
RIGHTS OF THE ABORIGINAL PEOPLES OF CANADA

35. (1) The existing aboriginal and treaty rights of the aboriginal peoples of Canada are hereby recognized and affirmed.

(2) In this Act, "aboriginal peoples of Canada" includes the Indian, Inuit and Métis peoples of Canada.

PART IV
CONSTITUTIONAL CONFERENCE

37. (1) A constitutional conference composed of the Prime Minister of Canada and the first ministers of the provinces shall be convened by the Prime Minister of Canada within one year after this Part comes into force.

(2) The conference convened under subsection (1) shall have included in its agenda an item respecting constitutional matters that directly affect the aboriginal peoples of Canada, including the identification and definition of the rights of those peoples to be included in the Constitution of Canada, and the Prime Minister of Canada shall invite representatives of those peoples to participate in the discussions on that item.

APPENDIX B

THE ROYAL PROCLAMATION
OCTOBER 7, 1763

RSC 1970, Appendices, pp. 123-29.

BY THE KING, A PROCLAMATION
GEORGE R.

Whereas We have taken into Our Royal Consideration the extensive and valuable Acquisitions in America, secured to our Crown by the late Definitive Treaty of Peace, concluded at Paris, the 10th Day of February last; and being desirous that all Our loving Subjects, as well of our Kingdom as of our Colonies in America, may avail themselves with all convenient Speed, of the great Benefits and Advantages which must accrue therefrom to their Commerce, Manufactures, and Navigation, We have thought fit, with the Advice of our Privy Council, to issue this our Royal Proclamation, hereby to publish and declare to all our loving Subjects, that we have, with the Advice of our Said Privy Council, granted our Letters Patent, under our Great Seal of Great Britain, to erect, within the Countries and Islands ceded and confirmed to Us by the said Treaty, Four distinct and separate Governments, styled and called by the names of Quebec, East Florida, West Florida and Grenada, and limited and bounded as follows, viz.

* * *

And whereas it is just and reasonable, and essential to our Interest, and the Security of our Colonies, that the several Nations or Tribes of Indians with whom We are connected, and who live under our Protection, should not be molested or disturbed in the Possession of such Parts of Our Dominions and Territories as, not having been ceded to or purchased by Us, are reserved to them, or any of them, as their Hunting Grounds.—We do therefore, with the Advice of our Privy Council, declare it to be our Royal Will and Pleasure, that no Governor or Commander in Chief in any of our Colonies of Quebec, East Florida, or West Florida, do presume, upon any Pretence whatever, to grant Warrants of Survey, or pass any Patents for Lands beyond the Bounds of their respective Governments, as described in their Commissions; as also that no Governor or Commander in Chief in any of our other Colonies or Plantations in America do presume for the present, and until our further Pleasure be known, to grant Warrants of Survey, or pass Patents for any Lands beyond the Heads or Sources of any of the Rivers which fall into the Atlantic Ocean from the West and North West, or upon any Lands whatever, which, not having been ceded to or purchased by Us as aforesaid, are reserved to the said Indians, or any of them.

And We do further declare it to be Our Royal Will and Pleasure, for the present as aforesaid, to reserve under our Sovereignty, Protection, and Dominion, for the use of the said Indians, all the Lands and Territories not included within the Limits of Our said Three new Governments, or within the Limits of the Territory granted to the Hudson's Bay Company, as also all the Lands and Territories lying to the Westward of the Sources of the Rivers which fall into the Sea from the West and North West as aforesaid.

And We do hereby strictly forbid, on Pain of our Displeasure, all our loving Subjects from making any Purchases or Settlements whatever, or taking Possession of any of the Lands above reserved, without our especial leave and Licence for that Purpose first obtained.

And, We do further strictly enjoin and require all Persons whatever who have either wilfully or inadvertently seated themselves upon any Lands within the Countries above described, or upon any other Lands which, not having been ceded to or purchased by Us, are still reserved to the said Indians as aforesaid, forthwith to remove themselves from such Settlements.

And whereas great Frauds and Abuses have been committed in purchasing Lands of the Indians, to the great Prejudice of our Interests, and to the great Dissatisfaction of the said Indians; In order, therefore, to prevent such Irregularities for the future, and to the end that the Indians may be convinced of our Justice and determined Resolution to remove all reasonable Cause of Discontent, We do, with the Advice of our Privy Council strictly enjoin and require, that no private Person do presume to make any purchase from the said Indians of any Lands reserved to the said Indians, within those parts of our Colonies where, We have thought proper to allow Settlement; but that, if at any Time any of the Said Indians should be inclined to dispose of the said Lands, the same shall be Purchased only for Us, in our Name, at some public Meeting or Assembly of the said Indians, to be held for that Purpose by the Governor or Commander in Chief of our Colony respectively within which they shall lie; and in case they shall lie within the limits of any Proprietary Government, they shall be purchased only for the Use and in the name of such Proprietaries, conformable to such Directions and Instructions as We or they shall think proper to give for that Purpose; And we do, by the Advice of our Privy Council, declare and enjoin, that the Trade with the said Indians shall be free and open to all our Subjects whatever, provided that every Person who may incline to Trade with the said Indians do take out a Licence for carrying on such Trade from the Governor or Commander in Chief of any of our Colonies respectively where such Person shall reside, and also give Security to observe such Regulations as We shall at any Time think fit, by ourselves or by our Commissaries to be appointed for this Purpose, to direct and appoint for the Benefit of the said Trade:

And we do hereby authorize, enjoin, and require the Governors and Commanders in Chief of all our Colonies respectively, as well those under Our immediate Government as those under the Government and Direction of Proprietaries, to grant such Licences without Fee or Reward, taking special Care to insert therein a Condition, that such Licence shall be void, and the Security forfeited in case the Person to whom the same is granted shall refuse or neglect to observe such Regulations as We shall think proper to prescribe as aforesaid.

And we do further expressly enjoin and require all Officers whatever, as well Military as those Employed in the Management and Direction of Indian Affairs, within the Territories reserved as aforesaid for the use of the said Indians, to seize and apprehend all Persons whatever, who standing charged with Treason, Misprisions of Treason, Murders, or other Felonies or Misdemeanors, shall fly from Justice and take Refuge in the said Territory, and to send them under a proper guard to the Colony where the Crime was committed of which they stand accused, in order to take their Trial for the same.

Given at our Court at St. James's the 7th Day of October 1763, in the Third Year of our Reign.

GOD SAVE THE KING

APPENDIX C
TREATY NO. 4

Articles of a Treaty made and concluded this fifteenth day of September, in the year of Our Lord one thousand eight hundred and seventy-four, between Her Most Gracious Majesty the Queen of Great Britain and Ireland, by Her Commissioners, the Honourable Alexander Morris, Lieutenant Governor of the Province of Manitoba and the North-West Territories; the Honourable David Laird, Minister of the Interior, and William Joseph Christie, Esquire, of Brockville, Ontario, of the one part; and the Cree, Saulteaux and other Indians, inhabitants of the territory within the limits hereinafter defined and described by their Chiefs and Headmen, chosen and named as hereinafter mentioned, of the other part.

Whereas the Indians inhabiting the said territory have, pursuant to an appointment made by the said Commissioners, been convened at a meeting at the Qu'Appelle Lakes, to deliberate upon certain matters of interest to Her Most Gracious Majesty, of the one part, and the said Indians of the other.

And whereas the said Indians have been notified and informed by Her Majesty's said Commissioners that it is the desire of Her Majesty to open up for settlement, immigration, trade and such other purposes as to Her Majesty may seem meet, a tract of country bounded and described as hereinafter mentioned, and to obtain the consent thereto of Her Indian subjects inhabiting the said tract, and to make a treaty and arrange with them, so that there may be peace and good will between them and Her Majesty and between them and Her Majesty's other subjects, and that Her Indian people may know and be assured of what allowance they are to count upon and receive from Her Majesty's bounty and benevolence.

And whereas the Indians of the said tract, duly convened in Council as aforesaid, and being requested by Her Majesty's said Commissioners to name certain Chiefs and Headmen, who should be authorized on their behalf to conduct such negotiations and sign any treaty to be founded thereon, and to become responsible to Her Majesty for their faithful performance by their respective bands of such obligations as shall be assumed by them the said Indians, have thereupon named the following persons for that purpose, that is to say: Ka-ki-shi-way, or "Loud Voice," (Qu'Appelle River); Pis-qua, or "The Plain" (Leech Lake); Ka-wey-ance, or "The Little Boy" (Leech Lake); Ka-kee-na-wup, or "One that sits like an Eagle" (Upper Qu'Appelle Lakes);

Kus-kee-tew-mus-coo-mus-qua, or "Little Black Bear" (Cypress Hills); Ka-ne-on-us-ka-tew, or "One that walks on four claws" (Little Touchwood Hills); Cau-ah-ha-cha-pew, or "Making ready the Bow" (South side of the South Branch of the Saskatchewan); Kii-si-caw-ah-chuck, or "Day-Star" (South side of the South Branch of the Saskatchewan); Ka-na-ca-toose, "The Poor Man" (Touchwood Hills and Qu'Appelle Lakes); Ka-kii-wis-ta-haw, or "Him that flies around" (towards the Cypress Hills); Cha-ca-chas (Qu'Appelle River); Wah-pii-moose-too-siis, or "The White Calf" (or Pus-coos) (Qu'Appelle River); Gabriel Cote, or Mee-may, or "The Pigeon" (Fort Pelly).

And thereupon in open council the different bands, having presented the men of their choice to the said Commissioners as the Chiefs and Headmen, for the purpose aforesaid, of the respective bands of Indians inhabiting the said district hereinafter described.

And whereas the said Commissioners have proceeded to negotiate a treaty with the said Indians, and the same has been finally agreed upon and concluded as follows, that is to say:—

The Cree and Saulteaux Tribes of Indians, and all other Indians inhabiting the district hereinafter described and defined, do hereby cede, release, surrender and yield up to the Government of the Dominion of Canada, for Her Majesty the Queen, and Her successors forever, all their rights, titles and privileges whatsoever, to the lands included within the following limits, that is to say:—

Commencing at a point on the United States frontier due south of the northwestern point of the Moose Mountains; thence due north to said point of said mountains; thence in a north-easterly course to a point two miles due west of Fort Ellice; thence in a line parallel with and two miles westward from the Assiniboine River to the mouth of the Shell River; thence parallel to the said river and two miles distant therefrom to its source; thence in a straight line to a point on the western shore of Lake Winnipegosis, due west from the most northern extremity of Waterhen Lake; thence east to the centre of Lake Winnipegosis; thence northwardly, through the middle of the said lake (including Birch Island), to the mouth of Red Deer River; thence westwardly and southwestwardly along and including the said Red Deer River and its lakes, Red Deer and Etoimaini, to the source of its western branch; thence in a straight line to the source of the northern branch of the Qu'Appelle; thence along and including said stream to the forks near Long Lake; thence along and including the valley of the west branch of the Qu'Appelle to the South Saskatchewan; thence along and including said river to the mouth of Maple Creek; thence southwardly along said creek to a point opposite the western extremity of the Cypress Hills; thence due south to the international boundary; thence east along the said boundary to the place of commencement. Also all their rights, titles and privileges whatsoever to all other lands wheresoever situated within Her Majesty's North-West Territories, or any of them. To have and to hold the same to her Majesty the Queen and Her successors for ever.

And Her Majesty the Queen hereby agrees, through the said Commissioners, to assign reserves for said Indians, such reserves to be selected by officers of Her Majesty's Government of the Dominion of Canada appointed for that purpose, after conference with each band of the Indians, and to be of sufficient area to allow one square mile for each family of five or in that proportion for larger or smaller families; provided, however, that it be understood that, if at the time of the selection of any reserves, as aforesaid, there are any settlers within the bounds of lands reserved for any band, Her Majesty retains the right to deal with such settlers as She shall deem just, so as not to diminish the extent of land allotted to the Indians; and provided, further, that the aforesaid reserves of land, or any part thereof, or any interest or right therein, or appurtenant thereto, may be sold, leased or otherwise disposed of by the said Government for the use and benefit of the said Indians, with the consent of the Indians entitled thereto first had and obtained, but in no wise shall the said Indians, or any of them, be entitled to sell or otherwise alienate any of the lands allotted to them as reserves.

In view of the satisfaction with which the Queen views the ready response which Her Majesty's Indian subjects have accorded to the invitation of Her said Commissioners to meet them on this occasion, and also in token of their general good conduct and behaviour, She hereby, through Her Commissioners, makes the Indians of the bands here represented a present, for each Chief of twenty-five dollars in cash, a coat and a Queen's silver medal; for each Headman, not exceeding four in each band, fifteen dollars in cash and a coat; and for every other man, woman and child twelve dollars in cash; and for those here assembled some powder, shot, blankets, calicoes, strouds and other articles.

As soon as possible after the execution of this treaty Her Majesty shall cause a census to be taken of all the Indians inhabiting the tract hereinbefore described, and shall, next year, and annually afterwards for ever, cause to be paid in cash at some suitable season to be duly notified to the Indians, and at a place or places to be appointed for that purpose, within the territory ceded, each Chief twenty-five dollars; each Headman, not exceeding four to a band, fifteen dollars; and to every other Indian man, woman and child, five dollars per head; such payment to be made to the heads of families for those belonging thereto, unless for some special reason it be found objectionable.

Her Majesty also agrees that each Chief and each Headman, not to

exceed four in each band, once in every three years during the term of
their offices shall receive a suitable suit of clothing, and that yearly and
every year She will cause to be distributed among the different bands
included in the limits of this treaty powder, shot, ball and twine, in all
to the value of seven hundred and fifty dollars; and each Chief shall
receive hereafter, in recognition of the closing of the treaty, a suitable
flag.

It is further agreed between Her Majesty and the said Indians that
the following articles shall be supplied to any band thereof who are
now actually cultivating the soil, or who shall hereafter settle on their
reserves and commence to break up the land, that is to say: two hoes,
one spade, one scythe and one axe for every family so actually cultivating, and enough seed wheat, barley, oats and potatoes to plant such
land as they have broken up; also one plough and two harrows for
every ten families so cultivating as aforesaid, and also to each Chief for
the use of his band as aforesaid, one yoke of oxen, one bull, four cows,
a chest of ordinary carpenter's tools, five hand saws, five augers, one
cross-cut saw, one pit-saw, the necessary files and one grindstone, all
the aforesaid articles to be given, once for all, for the encouragement
of the practice of agriculture among the Indians.

Further, Her Majesty agrees to maintain a school in the reserve
allotted to each band as soon as they settle on said reserve and are
prepared for a teacher.

Further, Her Majesty agrees that within the boundary of the Indian
reserves, until otherwise determined by the Government of the
Dominion of Canada, no intoxicating liquor shall be allowed to be
introduced or sold, and all laws now in force, or hereafter to be
enacted, to preserve Her Indian subjects, inhabiting the reserves, or
living elsewhere within the North-West Territories, from the evil
effects of intoxicating liquor, shall be strictly enforced.

And further, Her Majesty agrees that Her said Indians shall have
right to pursue their avocations of hunting, trapping and fishing
throughout the tract surrendered, subject to such regulations as may
from time to time be made by the Government of the country, acting
under the authority of Her Majesty, and saving and excepting such
tracts as may be required or taken up from time to time for settlement,
mining or other purposes, under grant or other right given by Her
Majesty's said Government.

It is further agreed between Her Majesty and Her said Indian
subjects that such sections of the reserves above indicated as may at
any time be required for public works or building of whatsoever
nature may be appropriated for that purpose by Her Majesty's
Government of the Dominion of Canada, due compensation being
made to the Indians for the value of any improvements thereon, and

an equivalent in land or money for the area of the reserve so appropriated.

And the undersigned Chiefs and Headmen, on their own behalf and on behalf of all other Indians inhabiting the tract within ceded, do hereby solemnly promise and engage to strictly observe this treaty, and also to conduct and behave themselves as good and loyal subjects of Her Majesty the Queen. They promise and engage that they will, in all respects, obey and abide by the law, that they will maintain peace and good order between each other, and between themselves and other tribes of Indians and between themselves and others of Her Majesty's subjects, whether Indians, Half-breeds, or whites, now inhabiting or hereafter to inhabit any part of the said ceded tract; and that they will not molest the person or property of any inhabitant of such ceded tract, or the property of Her Majesty the Queen, or interfere with or trouble any person passing or travelling through the said tract, or any part thereof, and that they will assist the officers of Her Majesty in bringing to justice and punishment any Indian offending against the stipulations of this treaty, or infringing the laws in force in the country so ceded.

In witness whereof Her Majesty's said Commissioners, and the said Indian Chiefs and Headmen, have hereunto subscribed and set their hands, at Qu'Appelle, this day and year herein first above written.

Signed by the Chiefs and Headmen within named in presence of the following witnesses, the same having been first read and explained by Charles Pratt:

W. Osborne Smith, *C.M.G.*
  Lt.-Col. D.A.G. Commg.
    Dominion Forces in North-West.,
Pascal Breland,
Edward McKay,
Charles Pratt,
Pierre Poitras,
       his
Baptist   x   Davis,
      mark
       his
Pierre   x   Denomme,
      mark
Joseph McKay,

Alexander Morris,
  Lt.-Gov. North-West Territories,
David Laird, *Indian Commissioner,*
William J. Christie,
          his
Ka-kii-shi-way,   x
          mark
         his
Pis-qua,   x
      mark
         his
Ka-wezauce,   x
       mark
         his
Ka-kee-na-wup,   x
        mark
              his
Kus-kee-tew-mus-coo-mus-qua, x
              mark
        his
Ka-ne-on-us-ka-tew,   x
        mark

Donald McDonald,

A. McDonald,
  Capt. Provl. Battn. Infantry,

Geo. W. Street,
  Ens. Provl. Battn. Infantry,

Alfred Codd, M.D.,
  Surgeon Provl. Battn. Infantry,

W. M. Herchmer, Captain,

C. de Couyes, Ensign,

Jos. Poitron, his x mark

M. G. Dickieson,
  Private Secy. Min. of Interior,

Peter Lapierre,

Helen M. McLean,

Flora Garriogh,

John Cotton, Lt. Canadian Artillery

John Allan,
  Lt. Provl. Battn. Infantry.

Can-ah-ha-cha-peu, his x mark

Kii-si-caw-ah-chuck, his x mark

Ka-wa-ca-toose, his x mark

Ka-ku-wis-ta-haw, his x mark

Cha-ca-chas, his x mark

Wa-pii-moose-too-sus, his x mark

Gabriel Coté or Mee-may, his x mark

APPENDIX D

A COMPARISON OF PROVINCIAL POWERS AND THE POWERS OF INDIAN BANDS UNDER THE INDIAN ACT

by

Donna Lea Hawley, L.L.B.

The British North America Act of 1867 (now called the Constitution Act, 1867) was drafted to ensure a strong federal government, with provincial government control over only local matters. Section 91 gave the federal parliament exclusive legislative jurisdiction over economic matters. The provincial legislatures (Section 92), were given control over social matters such as marriage, public health, local business, licences, the administration of justice, and property and civil rights. Section 93 added education as a provincial responsibility.

The federal parliament has, by section 91 (24), exclusive legislative jurisdiction over Indians and lands reserved for the Indians. The first Indian Act was passed one year following Confederation, and with infrequent revisions the present Indian Act creates local Indian governments with limited delegated authority.

The powers given to band councils are limited in one of two ways. The band must either obtain ministerial approval for actions it has taken, or it must request that the minister act on its behalf by making a regulation or order affecting the band in question. The powers of band councils are further restricted in that they cover only matters of a local or social nature. These powers closely parallel the powers granted to provincial legislatures under section 92.

The chart below compares provincial-government powers and band-council powers. Indian powers are divided into those that can be exercised by the band council, with confirmation and approval of the minister, and those that are exercised by the minister on behalf of the band.

COMPARISON OF PROVINCIAL-GOVERNMENT AND BAND-COUNCIL POWERS		
Provincial powers under 92 and 93 of Constitution Act 1867	*Band council powers under Indian Act*	*Ministerial powers for band under Indian Act*
92(1) repealed		

COMPARISON cont'd

92(2) Direct taxation for revenue	83(1) Taxing power of band	
92(3) Borrowing of money	70(1) Limited borrowing power	
	73(1) (m) Limited borrowing power	
92(4) Establishment and payment of provincial officers	74-80 Elections	
	2(1) Election by custom	
	83(1) (c) Officials	
	83(1) (d) Remuneration of council	
92(5) Management and sale of public lands and timber	81(g) Zoning	53-60 Management of reserves and timber
	81(i) Land allotment	
	38(1) Surrenders	
92(6) Establishment of prisons		
92(7) Establishment of hospitals	81(a) Provide for health	73(f) Spread of disease
		73(g) Health services
		73(h) Hospitalization
92(8) Municipal institutions		
92(9) Shop, saloon, tavern, auctioneer and other licences for revenue	81(h) Vendors	
	83(1) (a) (ii) Business licences	
	[98 Liquor laws on reserve]	
92 (10) Local works	81(f) Roads etc.	
	81(g) Zoning	
	81(h) Buildings	
	81(l) Public wells	

COMPARISON cont'd

	34 Roads and bridges	
92(11) Incorporation of companies		
92(12) Solemnization of marriage		
92(13) Property and civil rights	81(e) Cattle pounds	42-44 Descent of property
	81(g) Zoning	
		45-46 Wills
		48-50 Intestacy
		51 Mental incompetents
		52 Guardianship
		61-69 Band money
		73(1) (a)-(e), (h)-(l)
92(14) Administration of justice and courts	81(c) Law and order	
	81(d) Disorderly conduct	
	81(p) Trespass	
92(15) Punishment and fines	81(p) Trespass	103-108 Penalties
	81(r) Fines	
	81(1) (e) Fines	
92(16) Local matters	81(b) Traffic	
	81(j) Weed control	
	81(k) Bee keeping	
	81(m) Sports	
	81(o) Animals	
	81(q) Other	
93 Education		114-123 Education

It can be seen that bands have similar powers of self government as the provinces in eleven of the fifteen areas of control under Section 92. Power over education, however, is not given to the bands but is exercised by the minister (Section 93).

The federal government does not have the power to legislate the matters listed in Section 92. However, since it has complete legislative control over both Indians and Indian land, it may legislate on behalf of these people and lands in areas that are otherwise exclusively provincial, since provincial laws do not apply, without other authority, to Indians or Indian lands. Section 88 of the Indian Act states that all provincial laws that do not conflict with the Indian Act (or by-laws or regulations thereunder), treaties or other acts of parliament apply to Indians in the province. This extension of provincial laws does not apply to Indian lands.

The jurisdictional areas of legislative authority on reserve lands approximate those currently controlled by the provinces under Sections 92 and 93. The main difference between them is that the exercise of powers on reserves rests in the hands of the federal minister rather than a self-governing body. Thus it would be only a short step to transfer his authority to local Indian governments so that the latter would have legislative powers similar to those now held by the provinces.

APPENDIX E
DECLARATION OF THE FIRST NATIONS

A DECLARATION OF THE FIRST NATIONS

We the Original Peoples of this Land know
the Creator put us here.

The Creator gave us Laws that govern
all our relationships to live in harmony
with nature and mankind.

The Laws of the Creator defined our rights
and responsibilities.

The Creator gave us our spiritual beliefs,
our languages, our culture, and a place on
Mother Earth which provided us with all
our needs.

We have maintained our freedom, our
languages, and our traditions from time
immemorial.

We continue to exercise the rights and fulfill
the responsibilities and obligations given to
us by the Creator for the land upon which
we were placed.

The Creator has given us the right to
govern ourselves and the right to self-
determination.

The rights and responsibilities given to us
by the Creator cannot be altered or taken
away by any other Nation.

Assembly of First Nations Conference
December, 1980

Chief Charles Wood   Delbert Riley, President
Chairman, Council of Chiefs National Indian Brotherhood

APPENDIX F

METIS DECLARATION OF RIGHTS

DECLARATION OF RIGHTS

NATIVE COUNCIL OF CANADA — 1979

We the Metis and Non-Status Indians, descendants of the "Original People" of this country declare:

That Metis nationalism is Canadian nationalism. We embody the true spirit of Canada and are the source of Canadian identity.

That we have the right to self-determination and shall continue—in the tradition of Louis Riel—to express this right as equal partners in confederation.

That all Native people must be included in each step of the process leading to changes in the constitution of Canada.

That we have the right to guaranteed representation in *all* Legislative Assemblies.

That we have the inalienable right to the land and the natural resources of that land.

That we have the right to determine how and when the land and resources are to be developed for the benefit of our people and in partnership with other Canadians for the benefit of Canada as a whole.

That we have the right to preserve our identity and to flourish as a distinct people with a rich cultural heritage.

That we have the right to educate our children in our Native languages, customs, beliefs, music and other art forms.

That we are a people with a right to special status in confederation.

APPENDIX G

DENE DECLARATION

In Melville Watkins, *Dene Nation: The Colony Within,* 1977.

STATEMENT OF RIGHTS

We the Dene of the Northwest Territories insist on the right to be regarded by ourselves and the world as a nation.

Our struggle is for the recognition of the Dene Nation by the Government and peoples of Canada and the peoples and governments of the world.

As once Europe was the exclusive homeland of the European peoples, Africa the exclusive homeland of the African peoples, the New World, North and South America, was the exclusive homeland of Aboriginal peoples of the New World, the Amerindian and the Inuit.

The New World like other parts of the world has suffered the experience of colonialism and imperialism. Other peoples have occupied the land—often with force—and foreign governments have imposed themselves on our people. Ancient civilizations and ways of life have been destroyed.

Colonialism and imperialism are now dead or dying. Recent years have witnessed the birth of new nations or rebirth of old nations out of the ashes of colonialism.

As Europe is the place where you will find European countries with European governments for European peoples, now also you will find in Africa and Asia the existence of African and Asian countries with African and Asian governments for the African and Asian peoples.

The African and Asian peoples—the peoples of the Third World— have fought for and won the right to self-determination, the right to recognition as distinct peoples and the recognition of themselves as nations.

But in the New World the Native peoples have not fared so well. Even in countries in South America where the Native peoples are the vast majority of the population *there is not one country which has an Amerindian government for the Amerindian peoples.*

Nowhere in the New World have the Native peoples won the right to self-determination and the right to recognition by the world as a distinct people and as Nations.

While the Native people of Canada are a minority in their homeland, the Native people of the Northwest Territories, the Dene and the Inuit, are a majority of the population of the Northwest Territories.

The Dene find themselves as part of a country. That country is Canada. But the Government of Canada is not the government of the Dene. The Government of the Northwest Territories is not the government of the Dene. These governments were not the choice of the Dene, they were imposed upon the Dene.

What we the Dene are struggling for is the recognition of the Dene nation by the governments and peoples of the world.

And while there are realities we are forced to submit to, such as the existence of a country called Canada, we insist on the right to self-determination as a distinct people and the recognition of the Dene Nation.

We the Dene are part of the Fourth World. And as the peoples and Nations of the world have come to recognize the existence and rights of those peoples who make up the Third World the day must come and will come when the nations of the Fourth World will come to be recognized and respected. The challenge to the Dene and the world is to find the way for the recognition of the Dene Nation.

Our plea to the world is to help us in our struggle to find a place in the world community where we can exercise our right to self-determination as a distinct people and as a nation.

What we seek then is independence and self-determination within the country of Canada. This is what we mean when we call for a just land settlement for the Dene Nation.

This Declaration was passed at the 2nd Joint General Assembly of the Indian Brotherhood of the NWT and the Metis Association of the NWT on 19 July 1975 at Fort Simpson.

APPENDIX H

DECLARATION ON THE GRANTING OF INDEPENDENCE TO COLONIAL COUNTRIES AND PEOPLES

United Nations, General Assembly

The General Assembly of the United Nations, on December 14, 1960, adopted without a dissenting vote a "Declaration on the Granting of Independence to Colonial Countries and Peoples" in which it solemnly proclaimed "the necessity of bringing to a speedy and unconditional end colonialism in all its forms and manifestations."

By this decision of the General Assembly, which recognizes the "passionate yearning for freedom in all dependent peoples and the decisive role of such peoples in the attainment of their independence," the United Nations gave fresh impetus to the historic development which during the life of the Organization has seen more than 30 dependent territories, including four United Nations trust territories, gain sovereign independence and many others advance to the threshold of statehood. Despite the profound changes which have occurred during this period, some 50 million persons are living in non-self-governing territories which are still politically dependent on other countries. The full text of the Declaration is given below.

THE GENERAL ASSEMBLY,

Mindful of the determination proclaimed by the peoples of the world in the Charter of the United Nations to reaffirm faith in fundamental human rights, in the dignity and worth of the human person, in the equal rights of men and women and of nations large and small and to promote social progress and better standards of life in larger freedom,

Conscious of the need for the creation of conditions of stability and well-being and peaceful and friendly relations based on respect for the principles of equal rights and self-determination of all peoples, and of universal respect for, and observance of, human rights and fundamental freedoms for all without distinction as to race, sex, language or religion,

Recognizing the passionate yearning for freedom in all dependent peoples and the decisive role of such peoples in the attainment of their independence,

Aware of the increasing conflicts resulting from the denial of or impediments in the way of the freedom of such peoples, which constitute a serious threat to world peace,

Considering the important role of the United Nations in assisting the movement for independence in trust and non-self-governing territories,

Recognizing that the peoples of the world ardently desire the end of colonialism in all its manifestations,

Convinced that the continued existence of colonialism prevents the development of international economic cooperation, impedes the social, cultural and economic development of dependent peoples and militates against the United Nations ideal of universal peace,

Affirming that peoples may, for their own ends, freely dispose of their natural wealth and resources without prejudice to any obligations arising out of international economic cooperation, based upon the principle of mutual benefit, and international law,

Believing that the process of liberation is irresistible and irreversible and that, in order to avoid serious crises, an end must be put to colonialism and all practices of segregation and discrimination associated therewith,

Welcoming the emergence in recent years of a large number of dependent territories into freedom and independence, and recognizing the increasingly powerful trends towards freedom in such territories which have not yet attained independence,

Convinced that all peoples have an inalienable right to complete freedom, the exercise of their sovereignty and the integrity of their national territory,

Solemnly proclaims the necessity of bringing to a speedy and unconditional end colonialism in all its forms and manifestations;

And to this end

Declares that:

1. The subjection of peoples to alien subjugation, domination and exploitation constitutes a denial of fundamental human rights, is contrary to the Charter of the United Nations and is an impediment to the promotion of world peace and cooperation.

2. All peoples have the right to self-determination; by virtue of that right they freely determine their political status and freely pursue their economic, social and cultural development.

3. Inadequacy of political, economic, social or educational preparedness should never serve as a pretext for delaying independence.

4. All armed action or repressive measures of all kinds directed against dependent peoples shall cease in order to enable them to exercise peacefully and freely their right to complete independence, and the integrity of their national territory shall be respected.

5. Immediate steps shall be taken, in trust and non-self-governing territories or all other territories which have not yet attained independence, to transfer all powers to the peoples of those territories, without any conditions or reservations, in accordance with their freely expressed will and desire, without any distinction as to race, creed or color, in order to enable them to enjoy complete independence and freedom.

6. Any attempt aimed at the partial or total disruption of the national unity and the territorial integrity of a country is incompatible with the purposes and principles of the Charter of the United Nations.

7. All states shall observe faithfully and strictly the provisions of the Charter of the United Nations, the Universal Declaration of Human Rights and the present Declaration on the basis of equality, non-interference in the internal affairs of all states and respect for the sovereign rights of all peoples and their territorial integrity.

Published by United Nations Office of Public Information

Litho in U.N.   OPI/66—13187-June 1961-100M

APPENDIX I

INTERNATIONAL COVENANT ON THE RIGHTS OF INDIGENOUS PEOPLES*

PREAMBLE

The parties to the present covenant

Considering that the recognition of the inherent dignity and the equal and inalienable rights of individuals and of peoples is the foundation of freedom, justice and peace in the world, and considering that these principles are recognized and proclaimed in the Charter of the United Nations, the Universal Declaration of Human Rights, the International Covenant on Civil and Political Rights, the International Covenant on Economic, Social and Cultural Rights, the European Convention on Human Rights and the Inter-American Convention on Human Rights,

Conscious of the need for the creation of conditions of stability and well-being and peaceful and friendly relations based on respect for the principles of equal rights and self-determination of all peoples, and of universal respect for and observance of human rights and fundamental freedoms of all without distinction as to race, sex, language or religion,

Recalling that Convention 107 and Recommendation 104 of the International Labour Organization, 5th June, 1957, recognized the need for the adoption of general international standards to govern the relations between Indigenous Peoples and the states,

Recalling that the Declaration of the General Assembly on the Granting of Independence to Colonial Countries and Peoples. Resolution 1514 (xv), 14th December, 1960, recognized the ardent desire of the peoples of the world to end colonialism in all its manifestations,

Recalling that the inter-relationship of racial equality and decolonization was recognized in the Resolution of the General Assembly, Resolution 20166(xx) B, 15th December, 1965, associated with the

---

*Draft proposal adopted in Principle by the Third General Assembly of the World Council of Indigenous Peoples, May 1981.

adoption of the International Convention on the Elimination of All Forms of Racial Discrimination,

Considering that colonialism and the consequences of colonialism have not been eradicated for Indigenous Peoples, and, in consequence, Indigenous Peoples are frequently denied their political, economic, social and cultural rights,

Recognizing that the rights of Indigenous Peoples to self-determination is accepted in international law and has been increasingly given effect in the domestic law of States, and

Recognizing the long struggle by Indigenous Peoples to have their rights recognized in international law; agree on the following articles:

PART I
SELF-DETERMINATION

Article 1. All peoples have the right to self-determination. By virtue of that right Indigenous Peoples may freely determine their political status and freely pursue their economic, social and cultural development.

Article 2. The term Indigenous People refers to a people
   (a) who lived in a territory before the entry of a colonizing population, which colonizing population has created a new state or states or extended the jurisdiction of an existing state or states to include the territory, and
   (b) who continue to live as a people in the territory and who do not control the national government of the state or states within which they live.

Article 3. One manner in which the right of self-determination can be realized is—by the free determination of an Indigenous People to associate their territory and institutions with one or more states in a manner involving free association, regional autonomy, home rule or associate statehood as self-governing units. Indigenous People may freely determine to enter into such relationships and to alter those relationships after they have been established.

Article 4. Each state within which an Indigenous People lives shall recognize the population, territory and institutions of the Indigenous People. Disputes about the recognition of the population, territory and institutions of an Indigenous People shall initially be determined by the state and the Indigenous People. Failing agreement, such questions may be determined by the Commission of Indigenous Rights and the Tribunal of Indigenous Rights, as subsequently provided.

PART II
CIVIL AND POLITICAL RIGHTS

Article 1. Each Indigenous People has the right to determine the persons or groups of persons who are included within its population.

Article 2. Each Indigenous People has the right to determine the form, structure and authority of its institutions of self-determination. Those institutions, their decisions and the customs and practices of the Indigenous Peoples shall be recognized by domestic and international law on a basis of equality and non-discrimination.

Article 3. Where an Indigenous People exercise their right of self-determination within one or more states, and that state or states has some extent of jurisdiction over the Indigenous People or over individual members of the Indigenous People,

(a) the individual members of the Indigenous People are entitled to participate in the political life of the state or states on the basis of equality with citizens of the state or states,

(b) the Indigenous People is entitled to representation in the legislative and executive branches of government, the courts and civil service. The state is under an affirmative duty to promote that participation,

(c) it is recognized that it is desirable for the Indigenous People to have a national organization or organizations of their own choosing and structure, independent of the organs of the state, to represent their interests in dealing with the state. Where the poverty or dispersed character of the Indigenous People inhibit the development of such an organization or organizations, the state shall provide funding to the Indigenous People to facilitate the establishment and maintenance of such an organization or organizations.

PART III
ECONOMIC RIGHTS

Article 1. Indigenous Peoples are entitled to the lands they use and to the protection of the extent of use in areas where the use of land is shared in a compatible manner with others, and to those parts of their traditional lands which have never been transferred out of their control by a process involving their free consent.

Article 2. The need to protect the integrity of the lands of an Indigenous People is recognized. The land rights of an Indigenous People include surface and subsurface rights, full rights to interior and coastal waters and rights to adequate and exclusive coastal economic zones.

Article 3. All Indigenous Peoples may, for their own ends, freely use and dispose of their natural wealth and resources, without prejudice to any obligations arising out of international economic co-operation, based upon the principle of mutual benefit and international law. In no case may a people or a component unit of a people be deprived of its own means of subsistence.

Article 4. Where an Indigenous People have an economy reliant in whole or in part on hunting, fishing, herding, gathering or cultivation, they have the right to the territory and the waters used and needed for those pursuits. States are bound to respect such territories and waters and not act or authorize acts which could impair the ability of such lands and waters to continue in such use.

PART IV
SOCIAL AND CULTURAL RIGHTS

1. The cultures of the Indigenous Peoples are part of the cultural heritage of mankind. The shared beliefs of Indigenous People in co-operation and harmonious relations are recognized as a fundamental source of international law.

2. The primary responsibility for the protection and development of the cultures and religions of the Indigenous People lies with the Indigenous People. To this end the original rights to their material culture, including archeological sites, artifacts, designs, technology and works of art lie with the Indigenous People or members of the Indigenous People. Indigenous People have the right to reacquire possession of significant cultural artifacts presently in the possession of public or semi-public institutions, where possession of those artifacts was not obtained from the Indigenous People in a just and fair manner or where the artifacts are of major cultural or religious significance to the Indigenous People.

3. The Indigenous People have the right to fully control the care and education of their children, including the full right to determine the language or languages of instruction.

4. The Indigenous Peoples have the responsibility for the preservation and development of their languages. Their languages are to be respected by states in all dealings between the Indigenous People and a state on the basis of equality and non-discrimination.

PART V
RATIFICATION AND IMPLEMENTATION

Article 1. This Covenant shall be open to ratification by states and by Indigenous Peoples.

Article 2. To ensure the fulfillment of the provisions of this Covenant there shall be established a Commission of Indigenous Rights and a Tribunal of Indigenous Rights.

Article 3. The duties of the Commission of Indigenous Rights are:

(a) to receive and assess the reports of the states and of the Indigenous Peoples who are parties to this Covenant.

(b) to receive and assess petitions alleging the violation of the rights of Indigenous Peoples in contravention of the provisions of the present Covenant.

(c) to determine the appropriate recognition of the population, territory and institutions of an Indigenous People by a state, in compliance with Part I, Article 4.

(d) to investigate any petitions alleging the violation of the rights of Indigenous Peoples, with the power to require documents from states parties, with a right to access to officials of the states parties and with access to Indigenous lands, institutions and people within a state.

(e) to attempt to achieve a peaceful settlement of disputes involving Indigenous rights, by mutual agreement of the parties.

(f) to determine whether there has been a violation by any state or any Indigenous People of the provisions of the present Covenant.

(g) to conduct or commission research on matters of Indigenous rights, to conduct or support educational programs and to publish any reports, studies or determinations.

(h) to determine, in cases of dispute, the groups that are Indigenous People with a right of self-determination, subject to an appeal to the Tribunal of Indigenous Rights as subsequently provided. The Commission shall review all ratifications of the present Convention by Indigenous People to determine whether the ratifying group is an Indigenous People with a right of self-determination.

Article 4. The Commission will be composed of no fewer than 6 and no more than 19 persons. Each commissioner will be an Indigenous person of good moral character.

Article 5. Three persons will be nominated to the Commission from every state affected by the Covenant. A state is affected by the Covenant if

(a) it has ratified the Covenant, or

(b) an Indigenous People living wholly or partly within the state has ratified the Covenant.

Article 6. If a state has ratified the Covenant, or if an Indigenous People living wholly or partly within the state has ratified the Covenant, three Indigenous persons will be nominated by the most representative Indigenous organization or organizations in the state. The organization or organizations so qualified shall be designated by the Executive Council of the World Council of Indigenous Peoples. If sufficiently representative organizations do not exist, the Executive Council of the World Council of Indigenous Peoples shall designate an individual of the state to make all or some of the nominations.

Article 7. The members of the Commission shall be selected from the nominees by the Executive Council of the World Council of Indigenous Peoples, which shall also determine the number of Commissioners. Members shall serve terms of four years.

Article 8. The duties of the Tribunal of Indigenous Rights are to determine, after an investigation and determination by the Commission of Indigenous Rights:

(a) the groups which are Indigenous Peoples with a right of self-determination;

(b) any question of compliance with this covenant.

Article 9. A matter may be taken before the Commission by a state party, an Indigenous People party, the World Council of Indigenous Peoples or a person or persons affected by an alleged violation of the rights of an Indigenous People. A matter may be taken before the Tribunal, after the investigation and determination of the Commission of Indigenous Rights, by the Commission of Indigenous Rights.

Article 10. The Tribunal may request an advisory opinion from the International Court of Justice on any question of law arising in the course of its work.

Article 11. The Tribunal will hold public hearings and receive oral or written submissions. Parties may be represented by counsel. No rules of the Tribunal shall exclude any category of evidence.

Article 12. The Tribunal shall consist of up to 15 persons, 4 of whom will serve on a full-time basis. The members of the Tribunal may be Indigenous or non-Indigenous, shall be of good moral character and shall serve in their individual capacities.

Article 13. Each state party may nominate one candidate for the Tribunal. Each Indigenous People signatory to the present Covenant may nominate one candidate for the Tribunal. The members of the Tribunal shall be elected by secret ballot by the states and the Indigenous Peoples who have ratified the present Covenant. The elections will be conducted in a manner to ensure that a majority of the members of the Tribunal will be Indigenous people.

Article 14. The costs of the institutions created pursuant to the present Covenant shall be borne by the United Nations Organization.

Article 15. Nothing in the present Covenant may be interpreted as implying for any state, group or person any right to engage in any activity or perform any act aimed at the destruction of any of the rights recognized herein or at their limitation to a greater extent than is provided for in the present Covenant.

Article 16. There shall be no restriction upon or derogation from any of the rights recognized or existing in any state party to the present Covenant pursuant to law, conventions, regulations or custom on the pretext that the present Covenant does not recognize such rights or that it recognizes them to a lesser extent.

PART VI
REPORTING

Article 1. Each state and each Indigenous People which has ratified the present Covenant shall report to the Commission on Indigenous Rights every three years, describing fully the situation of the Indigenous People and the extent of compliance with the provisions of domestic and international law, including those of the present Covenant.

PART VII
COMING INTO FORCE

Article 1. The present Covenant is open for signature and ratification by any state and by any Indigenous People. Instruments of ratification shall be deposited with the Secretary-General of the United Nations.

Article 2. The present Covenant shall enter into force three months after the date of the deposit with the Secretary-General of the United Nations the sixth ratification by a state and the sixth ratification by Indigenous People. Until the establishment of the Commission of Indigenous Rights, the Executive Council of the World Council of Indigenous Peoples shall certify groups to be Indigenous People with a right of self-determination for the purposes of ratification of the present Covenant.

APPENDIX J

PROPOSED 1984 CONSTITUTIONAL ACCORD ON THE RIGHTS OF THE ABORIGINAL PEOPLES OF CANADA*

PART II.1
COMMITMENTS RELATING TO ABORIGINAL PEOPLES OF CANADA

35.2 Without altering the legislative authority of Parliament or of the provincial legislatures, or the rights of any of them with respect to the exercise of their legislative authority,

(a) Parliament and the legislatures, together with the government of Canada and the provincial governments are committed to
  (i) preserving and enhancing the cultural heritage of the aboriginal peoples of Canada, and
  (ii) respecting the freedom of the aboriginal peoples of Canada to live within their heritage and to educate their children in their own languages, as well as in either or both of the official languages of Canada;

(b) the aboriginal peoples of Canada have the right to self-governing institutions that will meet the needs of their communities, subject to the nature, jurisdiction and powers of those institutions, and to the financing arrangements relating thereto, being identified and defined through negotiation with the government of Canada and the provincial governments; and

(c) the government of Canada and the provincial governments are committed to participating in the negotiations referred to in paragraph (b) and to presenting to Parliament and the provincial legislatures legislation to give effect to the agreements resulting from the negotiations.

---

*Excerpted from a document tabled by the Prime Minister of Canada at the March 1984 meeting of the First Ministers' Conference on Aboriginal Rights.

APPENDIX K
A GUIDE TO FURTHER READINGS

The primary source of reading materials is found in the Bibliography. Here, I wish to supplement that source by suggesting readings on three topics not fully developed in the text.

ETHNOLOGY OF CONTEMPORARY NATIVE SOCIETY

The anthropological literature is replete with ethnographic accounts of contemporary Canadian native peoples. Virtually any of them will enrich the sketch of the Slavey economy used in Chapter 2 to indicate that autonomous native cultures still exist. The most complete ethnographic studies are found in the Mercury Series published by the Canadian Ethnology Service of the National Museum of Man. These monographs are free to the public and can be obtained by writing to the Service directly. Among the best examples are Guedon (1974) and Turner and Wortman (1977). However, the monographs are written in a highly technical manner, which might deter the general reader from wading through the anthropological lexicon.

Studies that are both scientifically accurate and linguistically accessible to the general public are harder to find. I would recommend four, however: Brody (1975, 1981), Tanner (1979) and Watkins (1977). The latter, although not an ethnography, contains contributions of an ethnological nature, both from academic and native sources. The result is a well-rounded picture of contemporary Dene society.

Shorter entries on contemporary native cultures appear in the Smithsonian Institution series *The Handbook of North American Indians*. Of the few volumes produced to date, one on the Canadian Subarctic (Helm 1981) is available and contains many useful items. As well, the *New Canadian Encyclopaedia* (forthcoming) contains brief entries on most Canadian native peoples, and sketch their contemporary culture as well as include guides for further reading.

NATIVE RIGHTS AND THE LAW

Chapter 4 focusses on aboriginal rights or, as I define them, rights that are founded on the recognition that aboriginal nations lived in societies prior to contact. Native rights is a much broader term, for it incorporates both aboriginal rights and those rights that derive from legislation, contract, treaty provisions or other explicit pronouncements by the state (sometimes as these have been interpreted by the courts). As well, aboriginal rights pertain to hunting, fishing and trapping and to property.

There is vast literature on the subject of native rights. The standard reference, although it was last republished in the early 1970s, is Cumming and Mickenberg (1972). Supplementary information is found in numerous articles that include Henderson (1980) on the question of usufructory rights; Bilsen (1976-77), Brown (1981), Cumming and Aalto (1973-74), Jordan (1978), Lysyk (1966), and Sanders (1973-74a and b) on hunting, fishing and trapping rights; and Hawley (1984) on the Indian Act. An important source for documents on native law is Smith (1975) and for the pre-Confederation treaties is Morris (1880). The text of post-Confederation treaties can be obtained by writing to the Department of Indian and Northern Affairs in Ottawa.

In recent years, the notion of aboriginal rights has become a focus of the legal literature. Among important recent interpretations are Green (1983), Lysyk (1982), Neidermeyer (1980-81), Manyfingers (1981), Sanders (1981, 1983) and Slattery (1982-83). Of crucial importance to the serious scholar are the extensively documented doctoral dissertations by Lester (1981) and Slattery (1979); each brings a breadth and scope to the analysis of the legal meaning of aboriginal rights, and both works will surely become the standard works upon which future interpretations will build.

RELATIONS BETWEEN NATIVE PEOPLES AND THE DESCENDANTS OF THE SETTLERS

Chapters 2, 4 and 5 all refer to this topic, but not in depth. For a historical account of the perceptions that the settlers and their descendants had of native peoples, the most informative source is Chamberlin (1975). For an exposition of that perception in the mid-nineteenth century, the best source is the detailed portrait of Thoreau's thought (respecting, among other writings, the ideas behind Walden) contained in Sayre (1973). Brown (1980), Innis (1956), and Ray (1974) provide excellent coverage of the role played by the fur trade in establishing economic and social relationships between native peoples and Europeans. A detailed examination of the process of treaty-making is contained in Fumoleau's (1975) account of Treaties 8 and 11. Recent books on Metis include the Metis Association's (of Alberta) 1981 publication on Metis land rights in Alberta; Flanagan (1983) on the life of Louis Riel; and Dobbin (1981) on Norris and Thomkins, who, in the 1930s and 40s worked to establish the Metis Association of Alberta. Tanner's volume of case studies (1983) provides interpretations of how native groups from different parts of

Canada interact politically with the Canadian state, whereas Adams (1975), Cardinal (1969) and Manuel and Poslums (1974) are accounts of such interactions, written by native people themselves. Dyck's (ed.) volume of essays (in press) provides a comparative perspective of native peoples' transactions with the liberal-democratic governments of Canada, Norway and Australia. Finally, Getty and Lussier (1983), in addition to informative articles on various aspects of Native Studies, includes an excellent bibliographic essay on "The Indian in Canadian Historical Writing, 1971-1981." This essay, together with Green and Sawyer (1983), provide an extensive list of current materials on Native Studies.

SUGGESTED READINGS

Adams, Howard
1975 *Prison of Grass.* Toronto: New Press.
Bilsen, Beth
1976-77 "Aboriginal Hunting Rights: Some Issues Raised by the Case of *R.V. Frank.*" *Saskatchewan Law Review* 41(1): 101-24.
Brody, Hugh
1975 *The People's Land: Eskimo and Whites – The Eastern Arctic.* Markham, Ontario: Penguin Books.
1981 *Maps and Dreams: Indians and the British Columbia Frontier.* Vancouver: Douglas and McIntyre.
Brown, Dougald
1981 "Indian Hunting Rights and Provincial Law: Some Recent Developments." *University of Toronto Faculty of Law Review* 39: 121-32.
Brown, Jennifer
1980 *Strangers in Blood: Fur Trade Company Families in Indian Country.* Vancouver: University of British Columbia Press.
Canadian Encyclopaedia, The
(forthcoming) Edmonton: Hurtig.
Cardinal, Harold
1969 *The Unjust Society: The Tragedy of Canada's Indians.* Edmonton: Hurtig.
Chamberlin, J.E.
1975 *The Harrowing of Eden: White Attitudes Toward Native Americans.* New York: Seabury Press.
Cumming, Peter A. and K. Aalto
1973-74 "Inuit Hunting Rights in the Northwest Territories." *Saskatchewan Law Review* 38(1): 252-323.
and Neil Mickenberg
1972 *Native Rights in Canada,* 2nd ed. Toronto: Indian-Eskimo Association of Canada and General Publishing.
Dobbin, Murray
1981 *The One-And-A-Half Men.* Vancouver: New Star Books.
Flanagan, Thomas
1983 *Riel and the Rebellion 1885 Reconsidered.* Saskatoon: Western Producer Prairie Books.
Dyck, Noel (ed.)
in press *Indigenous Peoples and the Nation-State: Fourth-World Politics in Canada, Australia and Norway.* St. John's, Nfld.: Institute of Social and Economic Research, Memorial University.
Fumoleau, Rene
1975 *As Long as This Land Shall Last: A History of Treaty 8 and Treaty 11, 1870-1939.* Toronto: McClelland and Stewart.

Getty, Ian and A.S. Lussier (eds.)

1983 *As Long as the Sun Shines and Water Flows.* Vancouver: University of British Columbia Press.

Green H. and D. Sawyer

1983 *The NESA Bibliography Annotated for Native Studies.* Vancouver: Tillacum Library.

Green, L.C.

1983 "Aboriginal Peoples, International Law and the Canadian Charter of Rights and Freedoms." *Canadian Bar Review* 61(1): 339-53.

Guedon, Marie-Francoise

1974 *People of Tetlin, Why are you Singing?* Ottawa: National Museum of Man. Mercury Series #9.

Hawley, Donna Lea

1984 *Indian Act Annotated.* Calgary: Carswell.

Helm, June

1981 *Handbook of North American Indians: Volume 6 Subarctic.* Washington: Smithsonian Institution.

Henderson, William B.

1980 "Canada's Indian Reserves: The Usufruct in Our Constitution." *Osgoode Hall Law Review* 12: 167-94.

Innis, Harold A.

1956 *The Fur Trade in Canada.* Toronto: University of Toronto Press.

Jordan, Anthony

1978 "Government, Two-Indians, One." *Osgoode Hall Law Journal* 16: 709-22.

Lester, Geoffrey S.

1981 "The Territorial Rights of the Inuit of the Canadian Northwest Territories: A Legal Argument." Unpublished Ph.D. dissertation. York University, Toronto.

Lysyk, Kenneth

1966 "Indian Hunting Rights: Constitutional Considerations and the Role of Indian Treaties in British Columbia." *University of British Columbia Law Review* 2(3): 401-21.

1982 "The Rights and Freedoms of the Aboriginal Peoples of Canada." In Walter S. Tarnopolsky and Gerald A. Beaudoin (eds.), *The Canadian Charter of Rights and Freedoms.* Toronto: Carswell. Pp. 467-88.

Manuel, George and Michael Poslums

1974 *The Fourth World: An Indian Reality.* Toronto: Collier-MacMillan.

Manyfingers, Wallace

1981 "Commentary: Aboriginal Peoples and the Constitution." *Alberta Law Review* 19(3): 428-32.

Metis Association of Alberta, *et al.*

1981 *Metis Land Rights in Alberta: A Political History.* Edmonton: Metis Association of Alberta.

Morris, Alexander
1880 *The Treaties of Canada with the Indians of Manitoba and the North-West Territories.* Toronto: Belfords, Clarke & Co. Reprinted 1979 Toronto: Coles Publishing.

Niedermeyer, Lynn
1980-81 "Aboriginal Rights: Definition or Denial?" *Queens Law Journal* 6: 568-86.

Ray, Arthur J., and Donald Freeman
1978 *"Give us Good Measure": An Economic Analysis of Relations Between the Indians and the Hudson's Bay Company Before 1763.* Toronto: University of Toronto Press.

Sanders, D.E.
1973-74a "Indian Hunting and Fishing Rights." *Saskatchewan Law Review* 38(1): 45-62.
1973-74b "Hunting Right—Provincial Laws—Application on Indian Reserves." *Saskatchewan Law Review* 38(1): 234-49.
1981 Aboriginal Peoples and the Constitution. *Alberta Law Review* 19: 410-27.
1983 "The Rights of the Aboriginal Peoples of Canada." *Canadian Bar Review* 61(1): 314-38.

Sayre, Robert F.
1973 *Thoreau and the American Indians.* Princeton: Princeton University Press.

Slattery, Brian
1979 "The Land Rights of Indigenous Canadian Peoples, as Affected by the Crown's Acquisition of their Territory." Ph.D. dissertation. Oxford University.
1982-83 "The Constitutional Guarantee of Aboriginal and Treaty Rights." *Queen's Law Journal* 8: 232-73.

Smith, Derek G. (ed.)
1975 *Canadian Indians and the Law: Selected Documents, 1663-1972.* Toronto: McClelland and Stewart.

Tanner, Adrian
1979 *Bringing Home Animals.* St. John's, Nfld.: Institute of Social and Economic Research, Memorial University.
1983 (ed.) *The Politics of Indianness: Case Studies of Native Ethnopolitics in Canada.* St. John's, Nfld.: Institute of Social and Economic Research, Memorial University.

Turner, David and P. Wortman
1977 *Shamattawa, the Structure of Social Relations in a Northern Algonkian Band.* Ottawa: National Museum of Man, Mercury Series #36.

Watkins, Melville
1977 *Dene Nation: The Colony Within.* Toronto: University of Toronto Press.

BIBLIOGRAPHY

Ahenakew, David
1983 Opening Remarks to the Constitutional Conference of First Ministers' on the Rights of Aboriginal Peoples. Ottawa. March 15, 1983.

Alberta Federation of Metis Settlements
1982 *Metisism: A Canadian Identity.* Edmonton: Alberta Federation of Metis Settlements.

Asch, Michael
1976 Addendum to the Submission of Michael Asch: Country Food Production. Records of the Mackenzie Valley Pipeline Inquiry. Government of Canada.

1977 "The Dene Economy." In M. Watkins (ed.), *Dene Nation: The Colony Within.* Toronto: University of Toronto Press, pp. 47-61.

1979 "The Economics of Dene Self-Determination." In David Turner and G.A. Smith (eds.), *Challenging Anthropology.* Toronto: McGraw-Hill Ryerson. Pp. 339-52.

1980 "Steps Towards the Analysis of Aboriginal Athapaskan Social Organization." *Arctic Anthropology* 17(2): 46-51.

1981 Field Trip Notes to the Shushwap of Alkali Lake, B.C. January, 1981.

1982 "Dene Self-Determination and the Study of Hunter-Gatherers in the Modern World." In Eleanor Leacock and R.B. Lee (eds.), *Politics and History in Band Societies.* Cambridge: Cambridge University Press. Pp. 347-72.

1983a "Native Research and the Public Forum." In Frank Manning (ed.), *Consciousness and Inquiry: Ethnology and Canadian Realities.* Ottawa: National Museums of Canada. Pp. 201-14.

1983b "Regard Anthropologique sur La Définition Judicaire des Droits Autochtones." *Recherches Amérindiennes au Québec* 13(3): 169-78.

Assembly of First Nations
1983 Proposals for Amendments and Additions to the Constitution Act, 1982. Unpublished manuscript.

Barsh, Lawrence Russel and J.Y. Henderson
1983 "Aboriginal Rights, Treaty Rights, and Human Rights: Indian Tribes and 'Constitutional Renewal.'" *Journal of Canadian Studies* 17(2): 55-81.

Benditt, Theodore M.
1982 *Rights.* Totowa, New Jersey: Rowman and Littlefield.

Bennett, Gordon
1978 *Aboriginal Rights in International Law.* London: Royal Anthropological Institute of Great Britain and Northern Ireland in association with Survival International.

Berger Thomas R.
  1977 *Northern Frontiers Northern Homeland: Volume II: Terms and Conditions.* Ottawa: Department of Supply and Services.
Black, Henry Campbell
  1968 *Black's Law Dictionary.* Rev. fourth ed. St. Paul: West Publishing.
Bodden, Kenneth R.
  1981 "The Economic Use by Native People of the Resources of the Slave River Delta." M.A. thesis, Department of Geography, University of Alberta.
Brody, Hugh
  1981 *Maps and Dreams: Indians and the British Columbia Frontier.* Vancouver: Douglas and McIntyre.
Canada. First Ministers' Conference on Aboriginal Constitutional Matters.
  1983a Unofficial and Unverified Verbatim Transcript. March 15, 1983. Vol. 1.
  1983b Unofficial and Unverified Verbatim Transcript. March 16, 1983. Vol. 2.
Challies, George S.
  1963 *The Law of Expropriation.* Montreal: Wilson and Lafleur.
Chamberlin, J.E.
  1975 *The Harrowing of Eden: White Attitudes Toward Native Americans.* New York: Seabury Press.
Claude, Richard P.
  1976 "The Classical Model of Human Rights Development." In R. Claude (ed.), *Comparative Human Rights.* Baltimore: Johns Hopkins University Press. Pp. 6-50.
Conner, Walker
  1973 "The Politics of Ethnonationalism." *Journal of International Affairs* 27(1): 1-21.
Cranston, Maurice (ed.)
  1966 *A Glossary of Political Terms.* London: Bodley Head.
Cumming, Peter and Neil Mickenberg
  1972 *Native Rights in Canada.* Second ed. Toronto: Indian-Eskimo Association of Canada and General Publishing.
Dacks, Gurston
  1981 *A Choice of Futures: Politics in the Canadian North.* Toronto: Methuen.
Dawson, R. MacGregor
  1970 *The Government of Canada.* Revised fifth edition. Toronto: University of Toronto Press.
Dene Nation (Indian Brotherhood of the NWT)
  1977 "The Dene Declaration." In M. Watkins (ed.), *Dene Nation: The Colony Within.* Toronto: University of Toronto Press. Pp. 3-4.

and the Metis Association of the Northwest Territories
 1982 *Public Government for the People of the North.* Yellowknife: The Dene Nation and the Metis Association of the Northwest Territories.
DIAND (Department of Indian Affairs and Northern Development)
 1969 *Statement of the Government of Canada on Indian Policy 1969.* Ottawa: Queen's Printer.
 1973 Statement on Claims of Indian and Inuit People. Press Release. August 1973.
 1975 *The Historical Development of the Indian Act.* Ottawa: Planning and Research Branch (of DIAND).
 1976 "An Approach to Government-Indian Relationship." Unpublished manuscript.
 1978 *Native Claims: Policy, Processes and Perspectives.* Ottawa: Queen's Printer.
 1981 *In All Fairness: A Native Claims Policy.* Ottawa: Queen's Printer.
Edward, P. (ed.)
 1972 *The Encyclopedia of Philosophy.* New York: MacMillan Company and The Free Press.
Feit, Harvey
 1982 "The Future of Hunters Within Nation-States: Anthropology and the James Bay Cree." In Eleanor Leacock and R.B. Lee (eds.), *Politics and History in Band Societies.* Cambridge: Cambridge University Press. Pp. 373-411.
Flanagan, Thomas
 1983a "The Case against Metis Aboriginal Rights." *Canadian Public Policy* 9(3): 314-25.
 1983b "Louis Riel and Aboriginal Rights." In Ian Getty and Antoine Lussier (eds.), *As Long as the Sun Shines and the Water Flows.* Vancouver: University of British Columbia Press.
Frelinghuysen, Thomas
 1977 "Speech Delivered in the Senate of the United States, April 7, 1830." In Anon. *Speeches on the Passage of the Bill for the Removal of the Indians.* Millwood, New York: Kraus Reprint Company. Pp. 1-30.
Frideres, James S.
 1983 *Native People in Canada: Contemporary Conflicts.* 2nd ed. Scarborough, Ontario: Prentice-Hall.
Green, L.C.
 1983 "Aboriginal Peoples, International Law and the Canadian Charter of Rights and Freedoms." *Canadian Bar Review* 61(1): 339-53.
Helm, June (ed.)
 1981 *Handbook of North American Indians: Volume 6: Subarctic.* Washington: Smithsonian Institution.
Higgins, Rosalyn
 1963 *The Development of International Law Through the Political Organs of the*

United Nations. Royal Institute of International Affairs. London: Oxford University Press.

Krech, Shepard
1980 "Introduction: 'Reconsiderations' and Ethnohistorical Reconstruction." *Arctic Anthropology* 17(2): 1-11.

Hughes, Christopher
1954 *The Federal Constitution of Switzerland*. London: Oxford University Press.

Legislative Assembly of the Northwest Territories
1977 Political Development Statement (untitled). Yellowknife, Northwest Territories.

Lester, Geoffrey S.
1981 "The Territorial Rights of the Inuit of the Canadian Northwest Territories: A Legal Argument." Unpublished J.D. dissertation. York University, Toronto.

House of Commons. Special Committee on Indian Self-Government
1983 *Indian Self-Government in Canada: Report of the Special Committee*. Ottawa: Queen's Printer.

Levi-Strauss, Claude
1969 *The Elementary Structures of Kinship*. Translated by Harle Bell *et al*. Boston: Beacon Press.

Lijphart, Arend
1977 *Democracy in Plural Societies: A Comparative Exploration*. New Haven: Yale University Press.

Lysyk, Kenneth
1973 "The Indian Title Question in Canada: An Appraisal in the Light of Calder." *Canadian Bar Review* 51: 450-80.

MacGowan, Kenneth and Joseph A. Hester, Jr.
1962 *Early Man in the New World*. Garden City, New York: Doubleday.

MacPherson, C.B.
1977 *The Real World of Democracy*. The Massey Lectures, Fourth series. Toronto: Canadian Broadcasting Corporation.

Maddock, Kenneth
1980 *Anthropology, Law and the Definition of Australian Aboriginal Rights to Land*. Nijmegen, Netherlands: Catholic University, Institute of Folk Law.

Manitoba Metis Rights Assembly
1983 "Manitoba Metis Rights Position Paper." Manitoba Metis Federation. Unpublished manuscript.

McRae, K.D.
1974 "Consociationalism and the Canadian Political System." In K.D. McRae (ed.), *Consociational Democracy: Political Accommodation in Segmented Societies*. Toronto: McClelland and Stewart: Carleton Library Series. Pp. 238-61.

Metis and Non-Status Indian Constitutional Review Committee
1981 *Native People and the Constitution of Canada.* Ottawa: Native Council of Canada.
Metis National Council
1983a Opening Statement to the Constitutional Conference of First Ministers' on the Rights of Aboriginal Peoples. Ottawa.
1983b The Rights of the Metis Peoples to be Entrenched into the Canada Act, 1982 Under Part II, Proposed Section 35.3. Ottawa.
Milne, David
1982 *The New Canadian Constitution.* Toronto: James Lorimer.
Morris, James
1973 *Heaven's Command: An Imperial Progress.* London: Penguin Books.
Murphy, Robert and Julien Steward
1956 "Tappers and Trappers: Parallel Processes in Acculturation." *Economic Development and Cultural Change* 4: 393-408.
National Indian Brotherhood
1973 Appendix "K" (Statement on Aboriginal Title) in Standing Committee on Indian Affairs and Northern Development 8: 42-44. Minutes of Proceedings and Evidence of the Standing Committee on Indian Affairs and Northern Development. Ottawa.
Native Council of Canada
1983 "Analysis Disputes Figures on Natives." Presented at First Ministers' Conference on Aboriginal Rights. Unpublished manuscript.
Nunavut Constitutional Forum
1983 "Building Nunavut: A Discussion Paper Containing Proposals for an Arctic Constitution. Government of the Northwest Territories, Yellowknife. Unpublished manuscript.
Ofvatey-Kodjoe, W.
1977 *The Principle of Self-Determination in International Law.* New York: Nellen.
Ormsby, William
1974 "The Province of Canada: The Emergence of Consociational Politics." In K.D. McRae (ed.), *Consociational Democracy.* Toronto: McClelland and Stewart. Pp. 269-74.
Pennock, J. Roland
1950 *Liberal Democracy: Its Merits and Prospects.* New York: Rinehart.
Ponting, J. Rich and Roger Gibbins
1980 *Out of Irrelevance: A Socio-Political Introduction to Indian Affairs in Canada.* Toronto: Butterworths.
Prime Minister's Office
1977 Press Release (August 3).
Report of the Mackenzie Valley Pipeline Inquiry
1977 *Northern Frontiers Northern Homeland: Volume II: Terms and Conditions.* Ottawa: Supply and Services.

Rushforth, Scott
1977 "Country Food." In M. Watkins (ed.), *Dene Nation: The Colony Within.* Toronto: University of Toronto. Pp. 32-46.

Sauser-Hall, George
1946 *The Political Institutions of Switzerland.* Zurich: Swiss National Tourist Office.

Sanders, Douglas
1978 "The Nishga Case." *The Advocate* 36(2): 121-36.
1983a "The Rights of the Aboriginal Peoples of Canada." *Canadian Bar Review* 61(1): 314-38.
1983b "The Re-Emergence of Indigenous Questions in International Law." In J. Anthony Long, M. Boldt, and L. Little Bear (eds.), *Aboriginal Rights: Toward an Understanding.* Lethbridge: University of Lethbridge.

Schmid, Carol
1981 *Conflict and Consensus in Switzerland.* Berkeley: University of California Press.

Senelle, Robert
1978 *The Reform of the Belgian State.* Brussels: Ministry of Foreign Affairs, External Trade and Cooperation in Development.

Slattery, Brian
1983 "The Constitutional Guarantee of Aboriginal and Treaty Rights." *Queen's Law Journal* 8: 232-73.
1979 "The Land Rights of Indigenous Canadian Peoples, as Affected by the Crown's Acquisition of Their Territory." Unpublished Ph.D. dissertation. University of Oxford.
1982-83 "The Constitutional Guarantee of Aboriginal and Treaty Rights." *Queen's Law Journal.* 8: 232-73.

Smith, Derek G.
1975 *Natives and Outsiders: Pluralism in the Mackenzie River Delta, Northwest Territories.* Department of Indian and Northern Affairs, Ottawa.

Smith, M.G.
1969 "Some Development in the Analytic Framework of Pluralism." In Leo Kuper and M.G. Smith (eds.), *Pluralism in Africa.* Berkeley: University of California Press. Pp. 415-58.

Staples, Janice
1974 "Consociationalism at Provincial Level: The Erosion of Dualism in Manitoba, 1870-1890." In K.D. McRae (ed.), *Consociational Democracy: Political Accommodation in Segmented Societies.* Toronto: McClelland and Stewart. Carleton Library Series #79. Pp. 288-99.

Steiner, Jury and R. Doerff
1980 *A Theory of Political Decision Modes: Intraparty Decision Making in Switzerland.* Chapel Hill, North Carolina: University of North Carolina Press.

Sutton, C. Gerald
1977 "Aboriginal Rights." In M. Watkins (ed.), *Dene Nation: The Colony Within*. Toronto: University of Toronto Press. Pp. 149-62.

Tanner, Adrian
1979 *Bringing Home Animals*. St. John's: Institute of Social and Economic Research, Memorial University of Newfoundland.

Tobias, John L.
1983 "Protection, Civilization, Assimilation: An Outline History of Canada's Indian Policy." In Antoine Lussier and I. Getty (eds.), *As Long as the Sun Shines and Water Flows: A Reader in Canadian Native Studies*. Vancouver: University of British Columbia Press. Pp. 39-64.

Trudeau, Pierre Elliott
1968 *Federalism and the French Canadians*. Toronto: Macmillan. Pp. 3-51.
1983 Opening Statement to the Constitutional Conference of First Ministers on the Rights of Aboriginal Peoples. Ottawa.

Tucker, St. George
1803 *Blackstone's Commentaries*. Philadelphia: William Young Birch and Abraham Small.

United Nations. General Assembly
1954 *Charter of the United Nations*. New York: United Nations.
1961 *Declaration on the Granting of Independence to Colonial Countries and Peoples*. New York: United Nations.

Upton, L.F.S.
1973 "The Origins of Canadian Indian Policy." *Journal of Canadian Studies* 8: 51-61.

Usher, Peter
1976 "Evaluating Country Food in the Northern Native Economy." *Arctic* 29(2): 105-20.
1980 "Renewable Resources in the Future of Northern Labrador: A Report to the Labrador Inuit Association." Ottawa, P.J. Usher Consulting Services. Unpublished manuscript.

Vincent, John M.
1891 *State and Federal Government in Switzerland*. Baltimore: Johns Hopkins Press.

Watkins, Melville
1977 *Dene Nation: The Colony Within*. Toronto: University of Toronto Press.

Weaver, Sally M.
1981 *Making Canadian Indian Policy: The Hidden Agenda 1968-1970*. Toronto: University of Toronto Press.
1983 "Federal Difficulties with Aboriginal Rights Demands." In J. Anthony Long, M. Boldt and L. Little Bear (eds.), *Aboriginal Rights: Toward an Understanding*. Lethbridge: University of Lethbridge. Pp. 87-98.

Yerbury, J. Colin
    1980 "Protohistoric Canadian Athapaskan Populations: An Ethno-
historical Reconstruction." *Arctic Anthropology* 17(2): 17-33.

CASES AND STATUTES

CASES

Baker Lake et al. v. Minister of Indian Affairs and Northern Development et al.
    [1980] 5 WWR 193, 50 CCC (2d) 377 (FCTD), (herein referred to as
    "Baker Lake").
Calder et al. v. Attorney General of British Columbia [1973] SCR 313, [1973] 4
    WWR1, 34 DLR (3d) 145, (herein referred to as "Calder 1973").
Calder et al. v. Attorney General of British Columbia [1970] 74 WWR 481
    (BCCA), (herein referred to as "Calder 1970").
Calvin's Case (1608) 7 Co Rep 1a, 2 State Tr 559, Moore KB 790, Jenk
    306, 77 ER 377.
In re Southern Rhodesia [1919] AC 210 (PC).
Kruger and Manual v. The Queen [1977] 4 WWR 300, [1978] 1 SCR 104, 75
    DLR (3d) 434, 14 NR 495, 34 CCC (2d) 377, (herein referred to as
    "Kruger").
Milirrpum et al. v. Nabalco Pty. Ltd. and the Commonwealth of Australia (1917),
    17 FLR 141 (SCNT), (herein referred to as "Milirrpum").
Regina v. Derriksan (1976), 31 CCC (2d) 575, [1976] 6 WWR 480, 71 DLR
    (3d) 159 (SCC).

STATUTES

The Constitution Act, 1982. Canada Gazette, Part III. 21 September,
    1982.
James Bay and Northern Quebec Agreement 1976. Québec: Editeur
    Oficiel du Québec.
Order of Her Majesty in Council Admitting Rupert's Land and the
    North-Western Territory into the Union. 23rd June, 1870. In RCS
    1970, Appendices: 257-77. Schedule A.
The Royal Proclamation, 1763. In RCS 1970, Appendices: 123-29.

INDEX

Aboriginal, defined, 5
Aboriginal people
    defined, 2, 5
    stereotypes, 13, 22-25
Aboriginal Rights
    Alberta, position, 7, 55
    and self-determination (*see* Self-
        determination)
    British Columbia, position, 48
    Assembly of First Nations, position,
        26-27, 28, 29, 34
    Baker Lake Case, 52-54
    Calder Case, 47ff, 64
    Coalition of First Nations, position,
        27, 89
    Constitution Act, inclusion, 1, 4, 89
    constitutional definition, 6-7
    defined, 7, 26
    existing, 5, 7, 8, 11 n.2
    federal government, position, 9,
        55-56, 65-68
    First Ministers' Conferences, dis-
        cussion, 7, 10, 27, 29, 55, 56, 71,
        87-88, 89, 105, 108 n.7
    Inuit Committee on National
        Issues, position, 27
    Metis National Council, position,
        27, 28
    Native Council of Canada, position,
        27
    Quebec, position, 55
Acculturation, 23-24, 25
Ahenakew, David, 28, 35, 89
Alberta Federation of Metis Settle-
    ments, 5
Amagoalik, John, 27
Apartheid, 75, 100-101, 106 n.3
Assembly of First Nations, 4, 26-27,
    28, 29, 34-36, 89
Assimilation, 62-63, 66, 68, 71, 76, 89,
    106 n.4

Baker Lake Case, 52-54
Beaver Indians, 20
British North America Act, 58, 83,
    105 n.4

Calder Case, 47ff, 64
Chartier, Clem, 28
Colonialism, 32-34, 37, 57
Comprehensive Claims Policy, federal
    government, 56, 65-66, 71
Consociational Constitutions
    aboriginal nations, proposals, 89-90
    defined, 77-78
    in Belgium, 77, 78-82, 83, 87, 90, 92,
        99, 101
    in Canada, 77, 82-87, 90, 106-107
        n.4
    in Switzerland, 77, 78-82, 83, 85, 87,
        108 n.6
    c.w. universalist constitutions, 76,
        77, 81
    c.w. apartheid, 100-101, 106 n.3
Constitution Act, 1867 (*see* British
    North America Act)
Constitution Act, 1982, 1, 2, 4,
Constitution, Canada, 1, 2, 4, 6-7, 8, 10
Cree, 20, 51, 59, 65, 68-70
Cultural relativity, 53, 54
Culture of poverty, 20, 22, 24

Dene, 6, 14-15, 16, 18-19, 24, 25 n.3,
    29, 69, 75, 90, 93, 96-99, 102, 105
Dene Declaration, 33, 35
Denendeh, 14, 93, 96-99, 102-103
Department of Indian Affairs and
    Northern Development, 62-63,
    65, 66-67, 68-69

Erasmus, Georges, 29
Eskimo (*see* Inuit)
Ethnocentrism, 42-43, 54
Ethnonational segmental autonomy
    (*see* segmental autonomy)
Ethnonational veto, 78, 80-82, 84-85,
    92

First Ministers' Conference, 1983,
    1, 2, 6-7, 10, 27, 29, 36, 40 n.6,
    55-56, 71, 88, 89
First Ministers' Conference, 1984,
    70, 108 n.7

Gosnell, James, 29

Hunting rights, 27, 47, 48, 52, 54, 58, 61, 66, 67, 71

Indian, 2, 3-4, 5, 9, 13, 26, 30, 59, 60-61, 62, 63, 65, 66, 91, 92
defined, 3, 4
non-status, defined, 4
status, defined, 4
Indian Act, defined, 3
Indian Association of Alberta, 89
Indian Policy of 1969, federal government, 8-9, 59, 63
Inuit, 2, 4, 5, 18, 20, 24, 26, 27, 30, 51, 53, 54, 66, 68, 90, 93, 94, 95, 102
defined, 4
Inuit Committee on National Issues, 26-27, 40 n.6
Inuvialuit, 65, 95-96

James Bay Agreement, 65, 68, 70

Liberal-democracy, 11, 72, 75, 76, 77, 78, 82, 88, 100, 101, 104
defined, 75, 76
Lougheed, Peter, 7

Mackenzie Valley Pipeline Inquiry, 10, 18
Manitoba, 63, 107 n.5
Manitoba Metis Association, 36
McGillivray, Don, 100, 101
Metis, 2, 3, 4, 5, 11 n.1, 26, 27-28, 30, 36, 63-64, 90, 91, 96-99, 102
defined, 5
Metis National Council, 26-27, 28, 34, 35, 36, 91
Montagnais-Naskapi, 20

Naskapi of Shefferville, 65
Native Council of Canada, 2-3, 26-27, 29-30, 36
Native economy, 15-22
Native Friendship Centres, 22
Northern Athapaskan-speaking Indians (*see* Dene)
Northwest Territories, 2, 14, 58, 65, 68, 69, 90, 93-95, 101-104

Nishga Case (*see* Calder Case)
Nishga Indians (*see* Calder Case)
Nunavut, 93, 94, 95-96

Original sovereignty, defined, 29

Quebec, 58, 68, 82-83, 85-86

Reciprocity, 21-22
Rights, defined, 6, 11
Royal Proclamation of 1763, 46-47, 50, 52, 57-58
Rupert's Land, 46, 52, 58

Salteaux, 59
Segmental autonomy (ethnonational), 78-80, 81, 83-84, 90-92
Self-determination, 1, 6, 11 n.3, 32-35, 38 n.3, 39 n.4
Self-government, aboriginal people
Assembly of First Nations, position on, 35, 36, 89, 91-93, 100
and apartheid, 75, 100-101, 106 n.3
Coalition of First Nations, position, 27
Dene Nation (Indian Brotherhood of the Northwest Territories), position, 40 n.6, 69, 96-99, 102, 103
Federal Government, position, 69-72, 108-109 n.7
House of Commons Special Commission on Indian Self Government, position, 70, 71, 90-93, 100
Inuit Tapirisat of Canada, position, 40 n.6, 69
Manitoba Metis Association, position, 36
Metis Association of the Northwest Territories, position, 40 n.6, 69, 96-99, 102, 103
Metis National Council, position, 34, 35, 36, 91-93, 100
Native Council of Canada, position, 34, 35, 36, 91-93, 100
N.W.T. 8th Legislative Assembly, position, 75

Nunavut Constitutional Forum,
    position, 94-96, 102, 103
provinces, positions, 108-109 n.4
    see Consociational Constitutions
Shuswap Indians, 20-21
Slavey, 14, 15-20, 25 n.4

Territorial acquisition
and colonialism, 31-32
Association of First Nations, posi-
    tion, 29
British definitions, 41-44
Dene Nation (Indian Brotherhood
    of the Northwest Territories,
    position, 29, 33
in Africa, 49

in Australia, 45-46
in Canada, 46-47, 50-51, 56-64
Native Council of Canada, position,
    29-30, 31
Trudeau, comment on, 31
Treaty 4, 59-62
Trudeau, Pierre E., 9, 10, 31, 64, 107
Two River, Bill, 89

United Nations, 32-33, 39 n.3, 4

White Paper of 1969 on Indian Policy
    (*see* Indian Policy)
Wilson, Bill, 29, 30, 31

Yukon Territory, 2, 58, 65